becoming a ux designer

A Comprehensive Guide to Launch Your UX Career

sarah michaels

contents

introduction

Definition and Importance of UX Design

Welcome to the fascinating world of User Experience (UX) Design! As you embark on this journey to become a UX Designer, it's crucial to understand the core principles that define the field and why it holds such significance in today's digitally-driven world. This section will introduce you to the essentials of UX Design, helping you build a strong foundation as you progress through the rest of the book.

At its core, UX Design is the process of creating products, services, or systems that are enjoyable, accessible, and efficient for users. The term "User Experience" encompasses all aspects of a user's interaction with a product, from the moment they first encounter it to the time they stop using it. UX Designers are responsible for shaping these experiences, ensuring that users find value and satisfaction in using the products they create.

But what does it mean to create a great user experience? UX Design is a multidisciplinary field that brings together elements of psychology, sociology, design, technology, and business. It involves understanding users' needs, preferences, and behaviors, as well as the context in which they use a product. By conducting research, UX Designers gain insights into users' goals, motivations, and pain points. These insights inform the design process, helping designers make informed decisions about the features, aesthetics, and interactions that will best serve their users.

The importance of UX Design cannot be overstated. In today's competitive market, where countless products and services vie for users' attention, a positive user experience can be the deciding factor in whether a product succeeds or fails. Users are more likely to engage with, and ultimately become loyal to, products that are easy to use, meet their needs, and provide a delightful experience.

To illustrate the significance of UX Design, let's consider a few real-world examples. When Apple introduced the iPhone in 2007, it revolutionized the mobile phone industry. The iPhone wasn't just a technological marvel; it was a triumph of UX Design. Its intuitive interface, sleek design, and seamless integration of hardware and software made it a pleasure to use, setting a new standard for smartphones and contributing to Apple's rapid rise in market share.

Similarly, the popularity of online platforms like Airbnb and Spotify can be largely attributed to their exceptional user experiences. Airbnb's platform simplifies the process of finding and booking accommodations, while Spotify's personalized recommendations and intuitive interface make it easy to discover and enjoy music. Both companies have built their success on the foundation of a well-crafted user experience, demonstrating the power of UX Design in driving customer satisfaction and business growth.

The value of UX Design extends beyond just consumer-facing products. In the realm of enterprise software, for example, poor user experiences can lead to lost productivity, increased training costs, and employee frustration. By prioritizing UX Design, companies can create more efficient, user-friendly tools that save time, reduce errors, and ultimately contribute to a better work environment.

As the digital landscape continues to evolve, the demand for skilled UX Designers is on the rise. Organizations across industries are recognizing the importance of UX Design in attracting and retaining customers, as well as improving their overall operations. As a UX Designer, you will have the opportunity to make a meaningful impact on people's lives by creating products and experiences that are not only functional but also delightful and engaging.

Throughout this book, you'll learn the skills, techniques, and principles needed to excel in this exciting field. From understanding user research and the design process to building a standout portfolio and navigating the job market, each section will provide you with valuable insights and practical advice to help you succeed in your journey to become a UX Designer.

As you continue reading, keep in mind that UX Design is an ever-evolving discipline. The best UX Designers are those who remain curious, adaptable, and committed to ongoing learning. Embrace the challenge of staying current with industry trends, emerging technologies, and new design methodologies. By cultivating a growth mindset and continuously refining your skills, you'll be well-prepared to tackle the diverse challenges and opportunities that await you in the world of UX Design.

In this section, we explored the definition and importance of UX Design, touching upon its multidisciplinary nature, real-world examples, and its impact on both consumer and enterprise products. We also highlighted the growing demand for UX Designers in today's competitive market. As you progress through the book, you'll delve deeper into the various aspects of UX Design, gaining a more comprehensive understanding of the field and the skills needed to excel in it.

Now that you have a foundational understanding of what UX Design is and why it matters, you're ready to embark on this exciting journey. The following sections will further explore the world of UX Design, guiding you through the process of developing your skills, building your portfolio, and launching your career in this rewarding field. Together, we'll help you unlock your potential as a UX Designer and empower you to create exceptional user experiences that make a lasting impact on people's lives.

overview of the ux design process

With a solid understanding of the definition and importance of UX Design, it's time to dive into the heart of the matter: the UX Design process. This section will provide you with a comprehensive overview of the various stages and activities involved in crafting user experiences. By understanding this process, you'll be better equipped to navigate your journey as a UX Designer and contribute meaningfully to the creation of delightful and effective products.

The UX Design process is a cyclical, iterative approach that involves understanding users, defining their needs, and designing solutions that address those needs. While there is no one-size-fits-all approach to UX Design, most processes share a set of core stages that guide designers in their work. These stages include:

Discover and Research   *PHASE EXPLORATION*

- The first stage of the UX Design process involves gathering information and insights about the users, their needs, and the context in which they will use the product. This stage typically includes activities such as:

- User interviews: Conducting one-on-one conversations with potential users to understand their needs, preferences, and pain points.

- Surveys and questionnaires: Collecting quantitative data from a larger group of users to identify trends and patterns.
- Market research: Investigating competitors, industry trends, and existing solutions to identify gaps and opportunities.
- Persona development: Creating fictional representations of user groups to help designers empathize with and better understand their target audience.

Define and Ideate   CONNECTIONS

- Once you have gathered sufficient information, the next step is to analyze the data and identify key insights that will inform the design process. This stage often includes activities such as:

- Affinity mapping: Grouping insights and observations to identify themes, patterns, and opportunities.
- Problem definition: Clearly articulating the specific problems or needs that the design should address.
- Ideation: Generating a wide range of potential solutions, leveraging creativity and collaboration to explore different design possibilities.
- Prioritization: Evaluating and selecting the most promising ideas to move forward with, based on factors such as feasibility, desirability, and impact.

Design and Prototype   REALISATION

- With a clear understanding of the problem and a set of potential solutions, the next step is to bring those ideas to life through design. This stage involves activities such as:

- Sketching and wireframing: Creating low-fidelity representations of the design to explore layout, hierarchy, and structure.
- Mockups and visual design: Developing high-fidelity designs that incorporate visual elements such as typography, color, and imagery.
- Prototyping: Building interactive models of the design that allow for testing and validation of the proposed solution.
- Design documentation: Creating detailed specifications that outline the design's features, interactions, and visual elements, to guide developers during implementation.

Test and Validate

- Before a design is implemented, it's crucial to ensure that it meets the needs of the users and addresses the identified problem. This stage includes activities such as:

- Usability testing: Observing users as they interact with the prototype, gathering feedback on the design's effectiveness and usability.
- A/B testing: Comparing different design variations to determine which one performs better in terms of user engagement and satisfaction.
- Analytics and data analysis: Examining usage data to identify patterns, trends, and potential areas for improvement.

- Iteration: Refining the design based on user feedback and testing results, making adjustments as needed to enhance the user experience.

Implement and Iterate

- The final stage of the UX Design process involves implementing the design and continuously refining it based on user feedback and performance metrics. This stage includes activities such as:

- Collaboration with developers: Working closely with development teams to ensure the design is accurately and effectively implemented.
- Quality assurance: Testing the implemented design for functionality, usability, and consistency with the intended
- Launch and monitoring: Releasing the product to users and monitoring its performance to gather insights and identify areas for improvement.
- Continuous improvement: Iterating on the design in response to user feedback, market changes, and technological advancements, ensuring the product remains relevant and effective.

As you can see, the UX Design process is an ongoing cycle of discovery, definition, design, testing, and iteration. This iterative approach allows designers to continually refine their solutions, ensuring that they remain aligned with user needs and expectations. By embracing this cyclical process, you'll be well-equipped to create user experiences that are not only functional but also engaging and delightful.

It's important to remember that while the stages outlined above provide a helpful framework for understanding the UX Design process, the specifics of each stage may vary depending on the project, organization, or designer. As you gain experience and develop your own unique approach to UX Design, you'll learn to adapt and customize the process to suit your needs and the needs of the projects you work on.

In this section, we've explored the key stages and activities involved in the UX Design process, from research and ideation to prototyping, testing, and iteration. With this overview in mind, you're now better prepared to delve deeper into each stage and develop the skills needed to excel as a UX Designer.

As you progress through the following sections, we'll dive into the specific techniques, tools, and strategies that will help you navigate each stage of the UX Design process with confidence. By building a strong foundation in the process and principles of UX Design, you'll be well on your way to creating exceptional user experiences that leave a lasting impact.

benefits of a career in ux design

Now that we've delved into the definition, importance, and process of UX Design, it's time to explore the many benefits of pursuing a career in this exciting field. From the personal satisfaction of creating impactful products to the diverse job opportunities and competitive compensation, there are numerous reasons why a career in UX Design may be the perfect fit for you. In this section, we'll discuss the key benefits of becoming a UX Designer and how this rewarding profession can lead to personal and professional growth.

/ Making a Meaningful Impact

1. One of the most fulfilling aspects of a career in UX Design is the opportunity to create products and experiences that genuinely improve people's lives. UX Designers strive to understand users' needs and

Tools for ARUN
Tools for URBAN DETIGN -
// for DRAWING

WORKSHOP

develop solutions that address their pain points, making everyday tasks more enjoyable and efficient. As a UX Designer, you'll have the chance to make a tangible difference in the world, contributing to the success of businesses and the satisfaction of their customers.

Creative Problem Solving

- UX Design is an inherently creative field that requires designers to think critically and inventively about the challenges they face. From brainstorming new features and interactions to refining the visual aesthetics of a product, UX Designers are constantly engaged in the process of creative problem-solving. If you're someone who thrives on innovation and enjoys the challenge of crafting unique solutions, a career in UX Design may be a perfect fit.

Diverse Job Opportunities

- The demand for skilled UX Designers is on the rise across industries, as businesses recognize the importance of user experience in driving customer satisfaction and loyalty. This growing demand translates to a wide range of job opportunities for UX Designers, from start-ups and tech giants to non-profits and government agencies. Additionally, UX Designers can specialize in various sub-disciplines, such as UX Research, Interaction Design, or UX Strategy, allowing you to hone your skills and pursue your unique interests within the field.

Competitive Compensation

- Along with the diverse job opportunities comes competitive compensation for UX Design professionals. As the demand for UX Designers outpaces the supply of qualified candidates, employers are increasingly willing to offer attractive salaries and benefits packages to attract top talent. While compensation can vary depending on factors such as location, experience, and industry, UX Designers generally enjoy above-average salaries compared to other professions.

Collaborative Work Environment

- UX Design is a highly collaborative field that often involves working closely with cross-functional teams, including product managers, developers, and marketers. This collaborative environment provides ample opportunities for learning, networking, and personal growth, as you'll have the chance to build relationships with professionals from various backgrounds and disciplines. If you enjoy working in a team-oriented environment and thrive on shared successes, a career in UX Design may be the right choice for you.

Dynamic and Evolving Field

- The world of UX Design is constantly changing, with new technologies, methodologies, and trends emerging regularly. This dynamic landscape offers UX Designers the opportunity to continually expand their skillsets and stay at the forefront of industry developments. If you're someone who enjoys lifelong learning and embraces the challenge of staying current in a rapidly evolving field, a career in UX Design can be both stimulating and rewarding.

Opportunities for Remote Work and Freelancing

- As digital tools and technologies continue to advance, more and more companies are embracing remote work and flexible working arrangements. This trend is particularly evident in the UX Design field, as many aspects of the design process can be conducted remotely using online collaboration tools. As a UX Designer, you may have the opportunity to work from home or pursue freelance projects, allowing for greater autonomy and flexibility in your career.

Having explored the many benefits of a career in UX Design, it's clear that this exciting field offers a wealth of opportunities for personal and professional growth. From making a meaningful impact on people's lives to enjoying diverse job opportunities and competitive compensation, there's no shortage of reasons why a career in UX Design might be the perfect choice for you.

As you consider pursuing a career in UX Design, it's essential to recognize that the field demands dedication, ongoing learning, and a strong commitment to understanding users and their needs. However, for those who are passionate about creating engaging and effective user experiences, the rewards of a career in UX Design can be immense.

In the sections ahead, we'll delve deeper into the specific skills and strategies needed to succeed as a UX Designer, guiding you through the process of building your portfolio, honing your techniques, and navigating the job market. As you continue on this journey, keep in mind the many benefits of a career in UX Design and the impact you can have on the world around you.

demand and job prospects for ux designers

As you've learned about the benefits of a career in UX Design, you might be wondering about the demand and job prospects for professionals in this field. In this section, we'll discuss the current job market for UX Designers, explore the factors contributing to the growing demand, and offer insights into the future of this exciting profession.

The demand for UX Designers has been steadily growing over the past decade, with companies across industries recognizing the critical role that user experience plays in the success of their products and services. This growing demand has led to a wealth of job opportunities for skilled UX professionals, as well as competitive compensation and attractive career prospects.

Factors Driving the Demand for UX Designers

1. There are several factors contributing to the increasing demand for UX Designers in today's job market:

- The rise of digital products: As more and more businesses shift their focus to digital platforms and services, the need for UX Designers to create engaging and effective online experiences has grown exponentially.
- Heightened consumer expectations: Today's consumers have high expectations for the products and services they use, and they're quick to abandon those that don't meet their needs. As a result, companies are investing heavily in UX Design to

ensure their offerings provide the seamless, enjoyable experiences that customers demand.

- Increased focus on customer satisfaction: Companies are increasingly recognizing that providing exceptional user experiences is crucial for customer satisfaction, loyalty, and long-term success. This recognition has led to a greater emphasis on UX Design within organizations, driving the demand for skilled professionals in the field.
- Digital transformation: As businesses undergo digital transformation, the need for UX Designers to help navigate this transition and ensure the seamless integration of digital products and services becomes paramount.

Job Opportunities for UX Designers

- The growing demand for UX Designers has led to a wide range of job opportunities across various industries and sectors. Some of the most common industries employing UX Designers include:

- Technology: UX Designers are in high demand within the technology sector, working for companies that create software, mobile apps, and other digital products.
- E-commerce: Online retailers rely heavily on UX Designers to create seamless shopping experiences that encourage customers to browse, purchase, and return for more.
- Finance: Banks, insurance companies, and other financial institutions are increasingly investing in UX Design to improve their digital platforms and provide better experiences for their customers.

- Healthcare: UX Designers play a crucial role in the healthcare industry, working to create user-friendly interfaces for medical devices, patient portals, and other digital tools.
- Government: As governments around the world digitize their services, there's a growing need for UX Designers to create accessible and user-friendly digital experiences for citizens.
- Non-profit organizations: UX Designers are also in demand within non-profit organizations, helping to create digital solutions that support the organization's mission and engage donors, volunteers, and beneficiaries.

Job Titles and Specializations

- Within the field of UX Design, there are numerous job titles and specializations that professionals can pursue based on their interests and skills. Some common job titles for UX Designers include:

- UX Designer: This generalist role involves working on all aspects of the UX Design process, from research and ideation to prototyping and testing.
- UX Researcher: Professionals who specialize in UX Research focus on gathering insights and understanding user needs through interviews, surveys, and other research methods.
- Interaction Designer: Interaction Designers concentrate on crafting the functional aspects of a product, such as navigation, transitions, and interactions between elements.
- Visual Designer: These professionals focus on the aesthetic aspects of UX Design, including

typography, color, and imagery, to create visually appealing and cohesive user experiences.

Future Job Prospects for UX Designers

1. As the digital landscape continues to evolve, the demand for UX Designers is expected to remain strong. Factors such as the ongoing digital transformation of businesses, the adoption of emerging technologies like artificial intelligence (AI) and virtual reality (VR), and the increased focus on inclusive design and accessibility will contribute to sustained growth in the field.
2. In addition to traditional UX Designer roles, new specializations and job opportunities are likely to emerge as the industry evolves. For example, UX Designers may find themselves working on voice user interfaces, designing experiences for wearable technology, or collaborating with AI engineers to create more personalized and adaptive user experiences.

With this bright outlook, it's clear that a career in UX Design offers not only a wealth of opportunities today but also the potential for continued growth and advancement in the future.

1 /
exploring the world
of ux design

ux versus ui design

AS YOU EMBARK on your journey into the world of user
experience (UX) design, you may have encountered the term
user interface (UI) design and wondered how these two disciplines relate to each other. Are they the same thing? If not,
what sets them apart? In this section, we'll dive into the
differences between UX and UI Design, explore how they
complement each other, and examine the unique skills and
responsibilities associated with each discipline.

Defining UX and UI Design

- To better understand the distinction between UX
  and UI Design, let's begin by defining each term:

- User Experience (UX) Design: As discussed in
  previous sections, UX Design is the process of
  creating products and services that provide
  meaningful, enjoyable, and effective experiences for
  users. UX Designers focus on understanding users'
  needs, motivations, and behaviors, using these

insights to inform the design of products that are both functional and engaging.

- User Interface (UI) Design: UI Design is the discipline of designing the visual and interactive elements of a product or service, including buttons, menus, forms, and other components that users interact with. UI Designers focus on creating aesthetically pleasing and accessible interfaces that facilitate seamless user interactions.

While UX and UI Design are distinct disciplines, they are closely related and often work hand-in-hand to create cohesive, user-friendly experiences. UX Design lays the foundation for an effective user experience, while UI Design builds upon that foundation to create an engaging and visually appealing interface.

The Key Differences between UX and UI Design

- Now that we have a basic understanding of what UX and UI Design are, let's examine some of the key differences between the two disciplines:

- Focus: The primary focus of UX Design is understanding and addressing the needs of users, while UI Design concentrates on creating visually appealing and accessible interfaces.
- Scope: UX Design encompasses a broader range of activities and responsibilities, including research, information architecture, and interaction design. UI Design, on the other hand, is primarily concerned with the visual design of interfaces and the presentation of information.

- Deliverables: UX Designers produce deliverables such as user personas, user flows, wireframes, and prototypes, while UI Designers create visual assets such as style guides, icons, and interface layouts.
- Tools: UX and UI Designers often use different tools to complete their work. UX Designers may use tools like Sketch, Figma, or Adobe XD for wireframing and prototyping, while UI Designers may rely on tools like Photoshop, Illustrator, or Affinity Designer for creating visual assets.

The Relationship between UX and UI Design

- Though UX and UI Design are separate disciplines, they are closely intertwined and often work together to create a cohesive and engaging user experience. In many cases, UX Designers and UI Designers collaborate throughout the design process, with UX Designers focusing on the overall structure and flow of the user experience, and UI Designers refining the visual and interactive elements of the interface.

In some organizations, UX and UI Designers may be separate roles, with each professional specializing in their respective discipline. In other cases, a single individual may be responsible for both UX and UI Design, depending on the size and scope of the project. Regardless of the specific roles and responsibilities, successful UX and UI Design relies on effective collaboration and communication between both disciplines.

Skills and Responsibilities in UX and UI Design

- While there is some overlap between the skills and responsibilities of UX and UI Designers, each discipline requires a unique set of expertise:

- UX Designer Skills and Responsibilities:
- Conducting user research and interviews
- Creating user personas and journey maps
- Developing information architecture and navigation systems
- Designing user flows and wireframes
- Creating and testing prototypes
- Collaborating with UI Designers, developers, and other team members
- Analyzing user feedback and iterating on designs
- UI Designer Skills and Responsibilities:
- Designing visually appealing and accessible interfaces
- Creating style guides and design systems
- Developing icons, buttons, and other interface elements
- Designing responsive layouts that adapt to different devices and screen sizes
- Collaborating with UX Designers, developers, and other team members
- Ensuring design consistency across all platforms and touchpoints
- Implementing designs using front-end development languages, such as HTML, CSS, and JavaScript (optional, but a valuable skill)

As you continue your journey into the world of UX Design, it's essential to understand the relationship between UX and UI Design and appreciate how these two disciplines complement each other. Whether you choose to specialize in one area or strive to become a versatile designer with expertise in both, remember that collaboration and communication are key to creating engaging and effective user experiences.

essential ux design principles

As you continue your journey into the world of UX Design, it's important to understand the fundamental principles that guide the design process. These principles serve as a foundation for creating user experiences that are engaging, enjoyable, and effective. In this section, we'll explore some of the most essential UX Design principles and discuss how they can be applied to your work.

User-Centered Design

At the heart of UX Design is the concept of user-centered design, which emphasizes the importance of placing users at the center of the design process. By focusing on the needs, preferences, and expectations of your target audience, you can create products and services that truly resonate with users and provide them with the experiences they desire.

To practice user-centered design, consider the following strategies:

- Conduct user research to gather insights into your target audience's needs, motivations, and behaviors.
- Develop user personas to represent different segments of your audience and guide your design decisions.
- Engage users in the design process by soliciting feedback, conducting usability tests, and iterating on your designs based on their input.

Consistency

Consistency is a key principle of UX Design, as it helps to create a sense of familiarity and predictability for users. By maintaining consistent design elements, such as typography, colors, and layout, you can make it easier for users to understand and navigate your product or service.

To ensure consistency in your designs, consider the following tips:

- Develop a style guide or design system that outlines the visual elements and interaction patterns to be used throughout your product.
- Reuse common interface components, such as buttons and menus, to create a cohesive experience across different screens and functions.
- Test your designs to ensure they maintain a consistent look and feel across different devices and platforms.

Clarity

Clarity is essential in UX Design, as it helps users to quickly understand how a product or service works and how they can interact with it. By presenting information in a clear, concise, and easy-to-understand manner, you can minimize user confusion and create a more enjoyable experience.

To enhance clarity in your designs, keep the following guidelines in mind:

- Use clear, straightforward language that is easily understood by your target audience.
- Organize information using headings, bullet points, and other visual cues to make it easier for users to scan and comprehend.
- Limit the number of interface elements and options presented to users at any given time to avoid overwhelming them.

Feedback

Providing users with feedback is a crucial component of UX Design, as it helps them to understand the consequences of their actions and feel more in control of their interactions. Feedback can be provided in various forms, such as visual cues, sounds, or vibrations, to communicate the results of user actions or the state of a system.

To incorporate effective feedback into your designs, consider the following suggestions:

- Use visual cues, such as highlights or animations, to indicate when a user has interacted with an interface element.
- Provide users with confirmation messages or alerts when they complete important tasks or make significant changes.
- Ensure that error messages are clear and informative, guiding users on how to resolve any issues they encounter.

Flexibility and Efficiency

A great user experience should be flexible and efficient, allowing users to complete tasks quickly and easily, regardless of their skill level or familiarity with a product. By designing for a wide range of users and providing multiple ways to accomplish tasks, you can ensure that your product or service meets the needs of a diverse audience.

To create flexible and efficient experiences, try implementing these strategies:

- Provide multiple ways for users to complete tasks, such as using menus, shortcuts, or voice commands.
- Design for different levels of user expertise by offering advanced features for experienced users

while keeping core functionality accessible to beginners.

- Optimize your designs for performance, ensuring that load times and response times are as fast as possible.
- Error Prevention and Recovery
- Errors are an inevitable part of any user experience, but UX Designers can take steps to minimize their occurrence and help users recover when they do happen. By designing with error prevention and recovery in mind, you can create more resilient and user-friendly products and services.

To minimize errors and support error recovery, consider these tips:

- Employ clear instructions and prompts to guide users through tasks and prevent errors from occurring in the first place.
- Implement error-checking and validation mechanisms to catch errors before they become critical issues.
- Provide clear error messages that explain the problem and suggest possible solutions, empowering users to correct their mistakes.
- Accessibility

- Accessibility is a crucial principle of UX Design, as it ensures that your product or service can be used by people with varying abilities and needs. By designing for accessibility, you can create inclusive experiences that cater to a wide range of users, including those with disabilities.

To design for accessibility, keep the following guidelines in mind:

- Ensure that your designs meet established accessibility standards, such as the Web Content Accessibility Guidelines (WCAG).
- Use clear, high-contrast colors and legible typography to make your content more readable for users with visual impairments.
- Design your interface to be operable using a variety of input methods, such as keyboards, touchscreens, or assistive devices.

As you continue your journey into the world of UX Design, strive to internalize these principles and apply them consistently across your projects. By doing so, you'll be well on your way to creating memorable and impactful user experiences that stand the test of time.

understanding user-centered design

As you delve deeper into the world of UX Design, one fundamental concept you'll encounter time and time again is user-centered design. This approach puts users at the forefront of the design process, ensuring that their needs, preferences, and expectations are prioritized and considered throughout each stage of development. In this section, we'll explore the user-centered design process, its benefits, and how to effectively implement this approach in your projects.

What is User-Centered Design?

User-centered design is a design philosophy that focuses on understanding and addressing the needs and goals of the end-users. This approach is built on the premise that a product or service should be designed with its users in mind, catering to their unique requirements and preferences to create an experience that is both functional and enjoyable.

The user-centered design process typically involves the following steps:

- Research: Conducting user research to gain insights into the target audience's needs, motivations, and behaviors.
- Analysis: Analyzing research findings to identify user goals, pain points, and opportunities for improvement.
- Design: Developing user personas, user flows, and wireframes to guide the design process.
- Prototyping: Creating interactive prototypes to test and refine the design.
- Evaluation: Assessing the usability and effectiveness of the design through user testing and feedback.

The Benefits of User-Centered Design

Implementing a user-centered design approach in your projects offers numerous benefits, including:

- Improved User Satisfaction: By focusing on the needs and preferences of users, you can create products and services that are more enjoyable, engaging, and effective.
- Increased Adoption and Retention: Users are more likely to adopt and continue using products that meet their needs and expectations.
- Reduced Development Costs: Identifying and addressing user needs early in the design process can help prevent costly redesigns and feature changes later on.

- Enhanced Accessibility and Inclusivity: Considering the diverse needs of your target audience ensures that your product is accessible and usable by a wider range of users.

Key Elements of User-Centered Design

To effectively implement a user-centered design approach in your projects, consider the following key elements:

- User Research: The foundation of user-centered design is a thorough understanding of your target audience. Conduct user research, such as interviews, surveys, and observations, to gather insights into their needs, motivations, and behaviors.
- User Personas: Develop user personas, or fictional representations of your target audience, to guide your design decisions and maintain focus on user needs throughout the design process.
- Empathy: Cultivate empathy for your users by understanding their perspectives, challenges, and goals. This helps you make more informed design decisions and create experiences that truly resonate with your audience.
- Iterative Design: Embrace an iterative design process, continually refining and improving your designs based on user feedback and testing. This approach allows you to fine-tune your product or service, ensuring that it meets the needs of users and provides an enjoyable experience.
- Collaboration: Involve stakeholders, such as developers, content creators, and other team members, throughout the design process. This collaborative approach ensures that user needs are considered across all aspects of the project,

resulting in a more cohesive and effective end product.

Implementing User-Centered Design in Your Projects

1. To successfully incorporate user-centered design in your projects, follow these steps:
2. Define your target audience: Before beginning the design process, identify the users who will be using your product or service. Consider factors such as demographics, motivations, and goals to develop a clear understanding of your audience.
3. Conduct user research: Use a variety of research methods, such as interviews, surveys, and observations, to gather insights into your target audience's needs and preferences.
4. Analyze research findings: Examine your research data to identify user goals, pain points, and opportunities for improvement. Use these insights to inform your design decisions and create experiences that cater to your users' needs.
5. Develop user personas and user flows: Create user personas to represent different segments of your target audience and guide your design process. Develop user flows to map out the steps and interactions users will take to achieve their goals within your product or service.
6. Design and prototype: Using the insights gained from your research, personas, and user flows, begin designing your product or service. Create wireframes and interactive prototypes to test and refine your designs.
7. Conduct user testing: Perform usability tests with real users to evaluate the effectiveness of your designs

and identify any areas that need improvement. Use the feedback you receive to iterate on your designs and further refine your product or service.

8. Implement and evaluate: Once you have a final design, collaborate with your team to implement the product or service. After launch, continue to gather user feedback and evaluate your product's performance, making any necessary adjustments to better meet user needs and expectations.

As you continue your journey into the world of UX Design, embrace the principles of user-centered design and strive to incorporate them into your work. By doing so, you'll be well-equipped to create memorable and impactful user experiences that truly resonate with your audience.

common ux design tools and technologies

As you embark on your journey to become a UX Designer, it's essential to familiarize yourself with the tools and technologies commonly used in the field. These tools can help streamline your design process, facilitate collaboration, and bring your creative visions to life. In this section, we'll explore some popular UX design tools and technologies, discussing their features, strengths, and applications.

Sketch

Sketch is a widely-used vector-based design tool, primarily for creating user interfaces and digital designs. Its simple, intuitive interface makes it easy for both beginners and experienced designers to work with. Some of Sketch's key features include:

- Artboards: Sketch allows you to create multiple artboards within a single document, streamlining your workflow and making it easy to manage complex projects.

- Symbols: Reusable components can be created using Symbols, ensuring consistency across your designs and speeding up the design process.
- Plugins: Sketch's extensive library of plugins lets you expand the tool's functionality, integrating with other apps and services to enhance your workflow.

Adobe XD

Adobe XD is another popular design tool, focused on creating user interfaces and interactive prototypes. It is part of the Adobe Creative Cloud suite, making it easy to integrate with other Adobe applications like Photoshop and Illustrator. Adobe XD's main features include:

- Auto-Animate: This feature allows you to create animated transitions between artboards, bringing your designs to life and making it easier to demonstrate interactions.
- Repeat Grid: The Repeat Grid tool enables you to create and edit lists and grids with ease, making it simple to design responsive layouts.
- Coediting: Adobe XD supports real-time collaboration, allowing multiple team members to work on the same document simultaneously.

Figma

Figma is a browser-based design and prototyping tool that supports real-time collaboration. Its cloud-based nature makes it easy to access your projects from any device, and you can work seamlessly with other team members. Some notable features of Figma include:

- Components: Figma's Components make it simple to create reusable UI elements, ensuring consistency across your designs and reducing design time.
- Multiplayer Editing: Figma allows multiple team members to work on the same document simultaneously, making collaboration effortless.
- Version History: Figma's built-in version control system lets you track and revert changes, ensuring you never lose your work.

InVision

InVision is a design collaboration and prototyping platform that integrates with popular design tools like Sketch and Adobe XD. It enables designers to create interactive prototypes, gather feedback, and collaborate with team members. Key features of InVision include:

- InVision Studio: InVision's desktop app, Studio, allows you to create responsive designs, animations, and interactions.
- Prototyping: InVision makes it easy to turn static designs into interactive prototypes, allowing you to test and iterate on your designs.
- Collaboration: InVision's commenting and annotation features make it simple for team members to provide feedback and collaborate throughout the design process.

Axure RP

Axure RP is a powerful design tool focused on creating wireframes, prototypes, and documentation for web and mobile applications. Its robust feature set allows you to create complex interactions and conditional logic, making it a popular choice for more advanced designers. Some of Axure RP's main features include:

- Dynamic Content: Axure RP's dynamic panels enable you to create interactive elements, such as accordions and carousels, without the need for coding.
- Conditional Logic: Implement conditional logic to simulate complex interactions and user flows.
- Adaptive Views: Design for different screen sizes and orientations with ease using Axure RP's adaptive views feature..

Balsamiq

Balsamiq is a rapid wireframing tool that allows you to create low-fidelity wireframes and mockups quickly. Its drag-and-drop interface and library of UI elements make it easy to sketch out ideas and iterate on designs. Some of Balsamiq's key features include:

- Sketch-like Interface: Balsamiq's sketch-like aesthetic promotes a focus on functionality and layout rather than visual design, making it ideal for early-stage design work.
- UI Library: Access a comprehensive library of pre-built UI components to speed up your design process.
- Collaboration: Balsamiq supports real-time collaboration, making it easy to work with teammates and gather feedback on your designs.

Marvel

Marvel is a design, prototyping, and collaboration platform that enables you to create interactive prototypes from static designs. It supports integration with tools like Sketch,

Adobe XD, and Figma, allowing you to bring your designs to life with ease. Marvel's main features include:

- Prototyping: Easily create interactive prototypes with Marvel's intuitive interface and pre-built UI components.
- User Testing: Conduct user testing directly within Marvel to gather insights and improve your designs.
- Handoff: Marvel's Handoff feature generates code, specs, and assets for developers, streamlining the transition from design to development.

Familiarizing yourself with these common UX design tools and technologies is an essential step in your journey to becoming a skilled UX Designer. Each tool offers unique features and strengths, so take the time to explore them and determine which one best fits your needs and workflow. As you become proficient in using these tools, you'll find that your design process becomes more efficient and enjoyable, allowing you to create exceptional user experiences that truly stand out.

industry trends and future developments

As a UX Designer, it's essential to stay informed about the latest trends and developments in the industry. By keeping up-to-date with new advancements, you can ensure that your skills remain relevant, and you continue to create cutting-edge user experiences. In this section, we'll explore some of the most significant industry trends and future developments in the world of UX Design.

The Rise of Voice and Conversational Interfaces

With the increasing popularity of voice-activated devices like Amazon Echo and Google Home, the demand for voice and conversational interfaces is growing rapidly. As a UX Designer, you'll need to understand how to design for these new types of interactions, considering factors like voice recognition, natural language processing, and user context. As these technologies continue to evolve, designers must adapt their approach to cater to this shift in user interaction.

Artificial Intelligence and Machine Learning

Artificial intelligence (AI) and machine learning have started to make significant impacts in various industries, including UX Design. These technologies have the potential to revolutionize the way designers work, automating tasks such as data analysis, user testing, and even generating design elements. By embracing AI and machine learning, UX Designers can create more personalized and dynamic user experiences, based on individual user preferences and behaviors.

Augmented Reality (AR) and Virtual Reality (VR)

AR and VR technologies are becoming increasingly mainstream, offering new and immersive ways for users to interact with digital content. As a UX Designer, you must understand how to design for these immersive environments, considering factors like spatial navigation, 3D UI elements, and user comfort. As AR and VR continue to advance, designers who can create compelling experiences for these platforms will be in high demand.

Inclusivity and Accessibility

In recent years, there has been a growing emphasis on designing for inclusivity and accessibility. This means creating user experiences that cater to a diverse range of users, including those with disabilities or impairments. As a UX Designer, it's essential to consider the needs of all users when designing your products, ensuring that your designs are accessible, usable, and enjoyable for everyone.

The Importance of Ethics in UX Design

As UX Designers, we have a responsibility to create products that not only provide a positive user experience but also do no harm. This includes considering the ethical implications of our design choices and prioritizing user privacy, security, and well-being. As the industry continues to evolve, designers must take a more active role in ensuring that their work aligns with ethical principles and promotes responsible technology use.

Remote Work and Collaboration

The shift towards remote work has transformed the way designers collaborate and communicate. Many UX Designers now work remotely, requiring the adoption of new tools and processes to facilitate effective collaboration. As remote work becomes more prevalent, UX Designers must adapt their workflows and embrace new methods of communication and collaboration to ensure seamless teamwork and project execution.

The Growth of Design Systems

Design systems are becoming increasingly popular as organizations recognize the value of having a consistent, scalable, and efficient approach to design. A design system is a comprehensive set of design guidelines, UI components, and processes that allow teams to create consistent user experiences across products and platforms. As a UX Designer, understanding how to create and work with design systems is essential for ensuring consistency, improving collaboration, and streamlining your design process.

Cross-disciplinary Collaboration

Another trend in the UX Design industry is the increased collaboration between various disciplines. Designers are now working more closely with developers, product managers, data scientists, and other stakeholders to create cohesive and well-rounded user experiences. As a UX Designer, it's essential to develop strong communication and teamwork skills, allowing you to work effectively with professionals from diverse backgrounds.

The Integration of UX Design and Business Strategy

UX Design is increasingly being recognized as a crucial component of business success. Companies are now looking to UX Designers to help shape their business strategies, ensuring that their products and services meet user needs and provide a competitive advantage in the market. As a UX Designer, it's essential to understand the business context of your work and consider how your design decisions impact broader organizational goals.

Personalization and Context-aware Design

As technology advances and the amount of user data available grows, there is a significant opportunity for UX Designers to create more personalized and context-aware user experiences. By leveraging data and insights about user behavior, preferences, and contexts, designers can create tailored experiences that adapt to individual user needs. As a UX Designer, it's important to understand how to work with data, incorporate user insights, and design for personalization while maintaining user privacy and trust.

To stay ahead in the rapidly evolving world of UX Design, it's crucial to keep learning and stay informed about the latest trends and developments. By embracing change, adapting to new technologies and methodologies, and continually honing your skills, you'll be well-positioned to thrive as a UX Designer in the years to come. Remember, the future of UX Design is as exciting as it is unpredictable, and being a part of this dynamic field means you'll never stop discovering new challenges and opportunities.

2 /
types of training and education

formal education

EMBARKING on a career in UX Design may leave you wondering about the role of formal education in your journey. While it's true that many successful UX Designers have forged their own paths through self-study and practical experience, formal education can provide a solid foundation and give you a competitive edge in the job market. In this section, we'll explore various formal education options, from undergraduate degrees to specialized programs, and discuss how they can help you build a strong foundation in UX Design.

Undergraduate Degrees

A bachelor's degree in a relevant field can be an excellent starting point for a career in UX Design. Many universities and colleges now offer degrees in areas such as Human-Computer Interaction, Interaction Design, or Cognitive Science. These programs provide a comprehensive education in the principles of design, human behavior, and technology, equipping you with the skills and knowledge needed to excel as a UX Designer.

Other undergraduate degrees that can be beneficial for a career in UX Design include:

- Graphic Design: Although UX Design goes beyond visual design, having a strong background in graphic design can be advantageous. Graphic design programs often teach foundational design principles, typography, and color theory, all of which can be applied in UX Design.
- Psychology: Since UX Design is focused on understanding and meeting user needs, a degree in psychology can provide valuable insights into human behavior, cognitive processes, and decision-making.
- Computer Science: A background in computer science can help you understand the technical aspects of UX Design, such as coding, algorithms, and software development processes.

Graduate Degrees

If you already hold a bachelor's degree in an unrelated field, pursuing a graduate degree in UX Design or a related discipline can help you transition into the field. Many universities offer master's and doctoral programs in areas like Human-Computer Interaction, Interaction Design, and Information Architecture. These programs typically provide advanced coursework in design theory, research methods, and usability, as well as opportunities to work on real-world projects and gain practical experience.

Bootcamps and Specialized Programs

Bootcamps and specialized programs are intensive, short-term training courses designed to provide hands-on experience in UX Design. These programs typically last several weeks to a few months and focus on teaching practical skills through project-based learning. Many bootcamps also offer career support services, such as job placement assistance, networking opportunities, and mentorship.

Some popular UX Design bootcamps and specialized programs include:

- General Assembly: Offers a full-time, 12-week UX Design Immersive program, as well as part-time, evening, and weekend courses.
- CareerFoundry: Provides a self-paced, online UX Design program with one-on-one mentorship and career support.
- Springboard: Offers an online, self-paced UX Design program that includes mentorship, real-world projects, and a job guarantee.

Online Courses and Certifications

There are numerous online courses and certification programs available for those looking to learn UX Design at their own pace. These courses cover various aspects of UX Design, from fundamentals to more specialized topics, and often include video lectures, readings, quizzes, and assignments. Some well-known platforms that offer UX Design courses and certifications include:

- Coursera: Features a range of UX Design courses, including a popular Interaction Design Specialization from the University of California, San Diego.
- Udemy: Offers a wide variety of UX Design courses, covering topics such as user research, wireframing, and prototyping.
- LinkedIn Learning: Provides a comprehensive library of UX Design courses, including a Learning Path that covers the essentials of UX Design.

Networking and Professional Associations

In addition to pursuing formal education, it's crucial to become an active member of the UX Design community. Attending industry events, conferences, and meetups can help you network with other professionals, stay informed about the latest trends and developments, and learn from industry experts.

You might also consider joining professional associations, such as the Interaction Design Association (IxDA) or the User Experience Professionals Association (UXPA). These organizations often offer valuable resources, such as workshops, webinars, and publications, as well as opportunities to connect with other UX Designers and industry professionals.

Building a Strong Portfolio

Regardless of the formal education path you choose, it's essential to develop a strong portfolio that showcases your skills, knowledge, and experience in UX Design. Your portfolio should include a diverse range of projects, demonstrating your ability to apply UX Design principles to various contexts and platforms.

As you work through your formal education, be sure to document your projects and collect artifacts, such as sketches, wireframes, prototypes, and research findings. These artifacts will help you create a compelling portfolio that demonstrates not only the final outcome of your work but also the thought process and problem-solving skills behind your designs.

Ultimately, the value of formal education in UX Design lies in its ability to provide a structured learning environment, access to experienced instructors, and opportunities for hands-on experience. While it's possible to succeed in the field without a formal degree or certificate, pursuing a structured educational program can help you build a strong foundation and accelerate your career growth.

As you navigate your educational journey, remember that learning is a lifelong process, and the most successful UX Designers are those who continually seek to expand their knowledge and skills. Embrace the opportunity to learn from your experiences, your peers, and the ever-evolving world of UX Design, and you'll be well on your way to a fulfilling and rewarding career.

bootcamps and online courses

As you embark on your journey to becoming a UX Designer, you might be wondering about the best educational route to take. Bootcamps and online courses are increasingly popular alternatives to traditional, formal education, offering flexible and focused training in a shorter timeframe. In this section, we'll dive deeper into the world of UX Design bootcamps and online courses, discussing their advantages, what to expect, and how to choose the right program for you.

The Appeal of Bootcamps and Online Courses

Bootcamps and online courses have gained popularity in recent years due to several advantages they offer over traditional educational programs. Some of these benefits include:

- Flexibility: Many online courses and some bootcamps allow you to learn at your own pace and on your own schedule, making it easier to balance your studies with work, family, or other commitments.
- Affordability: Bootcamps and online courses are often more affordable than traditional degree programs, reducing the financial burden of pursuing an education in UX Design.
- Practicality: These programs tend to focus on hands-on, project-based learning, allowing you to gain real-world experience and build a portfolio of work that demonstrates your skills to potential employers.
- Speed: Bootcamps and online courses can be completed in a matter of weeks or months, enabling

you to quickly gain the skills and knowledge needed to enter the workforce or make a career change.

Types of Bootcamps and Online Courses

There is a wide variety of bootcamps and online courses available, each with its own unique offerings and focus. Some common types of programs include:

- Full-time bootcamps: Intensive, immersive programs that typically last several weeks to a few months, requiring a full-time commitment. These programs often provide in-depth training, mentorship, and job placement support.
- Part-time bootcamps: Similar to full-time bootcamps but with a more flexible schedule, allowing you to continue working or managing other commitments while you learn. These programs often include evening and weekend classes.
- Self-paced online courses: These courses provide a flexible, asynchronous learning experience, allowing you to complete coursework and assignments on your own schedule. They may include video lectures, readings, quizzes, and projects.
- Online course series or specializations: A collection of related courses that, when completed together, provide comprehensive training in a particular area of UX Design. These series often include multiple courses, projects, and assessments.

Choosing the Right Program

With so many bootcamps and online courses available,

selecting the right program can be a daunting task. Here are some factors to consider when evaluating your options:

- Curriculum: Look for programs that cover the core principles and skills needed for a successful career in UX Design, such as user research, information architecture, wireframing, prototyping, and usability testing. Ensure the curriculum aligns with your goals and interests.
- Instructors: Research the backgrounds and expertise of the instructors, as their experience and teaching style can have a significant impact on your learning experience.
- Reviews and testimonials: Seek out reviews and testimonials from past students to gain insight into the quality of the program and the effectiveness of its curriculum.
- Networking and career support: Many bootcamps and online courses offer additional services, such as mentorship, networking events, and job placement assistance. These resources can be invaluable in helping you launch your career in UX Design.
- Cost and financing options: Consider the cost of the program and explore any financing options or scholarships that may be available. Keep in mind that investing in a quality education is likely to pay off in the long run, but it's essential to choose a program that aligns with your budget.

1. Making the Most of Your Bootcamp or Online Course Experience

Once you've chosen the right bootcamp or online course for you, it's essential to make the most of your learning experience. Here are some tips to help you succeed:

- Engage fully: Approach your studies with curiosity and dedication. Actively participate in discussions, complete assignments, and seek feedback from instructors and peers to enhance your understanding of the material.
- Apply your learning: Apply the concepts and techniques you learn to real-world projects, either by working on assignments within the course or by creating your own side projects. This will help you build a strong portfolio and reinforce your understanding of the material.
- Network with peers and professionals: Take advantage of any networking opportunities provided by your program, such as online forums, meetups, or conferences. Building connections with fellow students and industry professionals can lead to valuable collaborations, mentorships, and job opportunities.
- Seek additional resources: Supplement your learning with additional resources, such as books, articles, podcasts, and blogs, to deepen your understanding of UX Design and stay informed about industry trends.
- Reflect on your progress: Regularly assess your progress and accomplishments throughout the course, and use this information to set goals for further growth and development.

1. Transitioning to a UX Design Career

Upon completing your bootcamp or online course, you'll likely be eager to put your newfound skills to use and begin your career in UX Design. Here are some steps to help you make a successful transition:

- Update your resume: Highlight your UX Design skills, relevant coursework, and any projects you've completed during your program. Be sure to emphasize the impact and results of your work.
- Build a strong portfolio: Create a professional portfolio website that showcases your best work, including artifacts like wireframes, prototypes, and research findings. Your portfolio should tell a story about your design process and problem-solving abilities.
- Leverage your network: Reach out to your connections from your bootcamp or online course, including instructors, mentors, and peers, for advice, job leads, or referrals. Attend industry events and join professional associations to continue building your network.
- Apply for internships or entry-level positions: Gain practical experience by applying for internships or entry-level roles in UX Design. This will provide you with valuable on-the-job training and help you build a strong professional reputation.

self-study and online resources

While formal education, bootcamps, and online courses are all valuable paths to becoming a UX Designer, self-study can also be an effective approach for those who prefer a more independent learning experience. In this section, we'll explore the benefits of self-study, provide guidance on structuring your learning journey, and introduce a variety of online resources to help you build your skills and knowledge in UX Design.

The Benefits of Self-study

Self-study offers several advantages for aspiring UX Designers, including:

- Flexibility: Self-study allows you to learn at your own pace and on your own schedule, making it an ideal option for those with work, family, or other commitments.
- Customization: By choosing your own learning materials and resources, you can tailor your education to your specific interests and goals, focusing on the areas that are most relevant to your desired career path.
- Cost-effectiveness: Many online resources are available for free or at a low cost, making self-study an affordable option for building your UX Design skills and knowledge.
- Autonomy: Self-study fosters a sense of independence and self-reliance, empowering you to take charge of your own learning and growth.

Structuring Your Self-study Journey

While self-study offers considerable freedom and flexibility, it's essential to create a structured learning plan to ensure your efforts are focused and effective. Here are some steps to help you get started:

- Define your goals: Begin by identifying your specific goals and objectives for your self-study journey. What skills do you want to develop? What knowledge areas do you want to explore? Having clear goals will help you choose the most appropriate resources and stay motivated throughout your learning journey.
- Research the field: Familiarize yourself with the core principles, techniques, and tools used in UX Design. This will provide you with a solid foundation for selecting relevant learning resources and evaluating their quality and relevance.

- Create a learning plan: Develop a timeline and a list of resources to guide your self-study journey. Include a mix of books, articles, videos, tutorials, and projects to ensure a well-rounded learning experience.
- Set a schedule: Establish a regular study schedule that allows for consistent progress while still accommodating your other commitments. Dedicate specific blocks of time each week to focus on your self-study, and treat these sessions as non-negotiable appointments with yourself.
- Track your progress: Regularly review your progress and adjust your learning plan as needed. Celebrate your achievements, and use setbacks as opportunities for growth and reflection.

Online Resources for Self-study

There is a wealth of online resources available to support your self-study journey in UX Design. Some key categories of resources include:

- Online tutorials and courses: Many websites offer free or low-cost tutorials and courses in UX Design, covering topics such as user research, information architecture, wireframing, prototyping, and usability testing. Examples include Coursera, Udemy, LinkedIn Learning, and Skillshare.
- Blogs and articles: Stay up-to-date on industry trends and best practices by following UX Design blogs and reading articles by industry experts. Some popular UX Design blogs include Nielsen Norman Group, UX Collective, UX Design.cc, and Smashing Magazine.
- Videos and webinars: Watching videos and webinars can provide visual demonstrations of UX

Design techniques and tools, as well as insights from industry professionals. Look for content on platforms like YouTube, Vimeo, and UX Design conference websites.

- Books and e-books: Books can provide in-depth coverage of UX Design principles and practices. Some essential titles include "Don't Make Me Think" by Steve Krug, "The Design of Everyday Things" by Don Norman, and "About Face: The Essentials of Interaction Design" by Alan Cooper. Many books are available in both print and e-book formats, allowing you to choose the format that best suits your preferences and needs.
- Podcasts: Listening to UX Design podcasts can help you stay informed about industry trends, learn from interviews with professionals, and gain insights into real-world projects and challenges. Some popular UX Design podcasts include UX Podcast, The UX World, and User Defenders.
- Online communities and forums: Joining online communities and forums can provide opportunities for networking, collaboration, and mentorship, as well as access to valuable advice and resources. Examples include UX Mastery Community, Designer Hangout, and the UX Design subreddit.
- Tools and software: Familiarize yourself with the tools and software commonly used by UX Designers, such as Sketch, Figma, Adobe XD, and InVision. Many of these tools offer free trials, tutorials, and documentation to help you learn their features and capabilities.

- Tips for Successful Self-study

To make the most of your self-study journey, consider the

following tips:

- Stay curious: Approach your self-study with an open mind and a willingness to explore new ideas and perspectives. This curiosity will help you stay engaged and motivated throughout your learning journey.
- Be persistent: Learning UX Design can be challenging, and you may encounter setbacks along the way. Embrace these challenges as opportunities for growth, and remain persistent in your efforts to achieve your goals.
- Collaborate with others: Connect with other self-study learners or UX Design professionals through online communities, meetups, or social media. Sharing your experiences, challenges, and successes can provide valuable support and encouragement.
- Seek feedback: Regularly solicit feedback on your work from peers, mentors, or industry professionals. Constructive criticism can help you identify areas for improvement and enhance your skills.
- Apply your learning: Apply the concepts and techniques you learn to real-world projects, either by working on assignments within the course or by creating your own side projects. This will help you build a strong portfolio and reinforce your understanding of the material.

In this digital age, there are virtually limitless resources available for those who wish to pursue a self-study approach to UX Design. By leveraging these resources, creating a structured learning plan, and remaining committed to your goals, you can build a solid foundation in UX Design and embark on a rewarding career in this dynamic and growing field.

3 /
making a career switch to ux design

assessing your current skills and experience

AS YOU EMBARK on your journey to become a UX Designer, it's essential to take stock of your current skills and experience. By understanding your strengths and identifying areas for improvement, you can create a more targeted and effective learning plan that meets your unique needs and goals. In this section, we'll discuss the importance of self-assessment, offer guidance on evaluating your skills and experience, and provide strategies for leveraging your existing expertise to accelerate your transition into the world of UX Design.

- The Importance of Self-assessment

Self-assessment is a crucial step in your UX Design journey for several reasons:

- Identifying strengths: Recognizing your existing skills and strengths can help you build confidence and motivation, as well as pinpoint areas where you can leverage your expertise to excel in your new career.

- Uncovering gaps: Assessing your skills and experience can also help you identify gaps in your knowledge or abilities, allowing you to prioritize and target your learning efforts more effectively.
- Guiding your learning: A thorough self-assessment can provide valuable insights that inform your choice of educational resources, ensuring you select the most relevant and beneficial materials for your needs.
- Setting realistic goals: By understanding your current abilities, you can set achievable goals that align with your desired career path, helping to keep you motivated and focused throughout your learning journey.

Evaluating Your Skills and Experience

To assess your current skills and experience, consider the following steps:

- Review the fundamentals: Begin by evaluating your understanding of the core principles and concepts of UX Design, such as user-centered design, usability, information architecture, and interaction design. Determine whether you have a solid grasp of these fundamentals or if you need to invest time in building a stronger foundation.
- Assess technical skills: UX Designers often work with various tools and software to create wireframes, prototypes, and other design artifacts. Consider your proficiency in popular design tools like Sketch, Figma, or Adobe XD, as well as your ability to code in HTML, CSS, and JavaScript, if applicable.

- Evaluate soft skills: Soft skills, such as communication, collaboration, problem-solving, and empathy, play a crucial role in UX Design. Reflect on your strengths and weaknesses in these areas and consider ways to enhance your abilities.
- Reflect on related experience: Consider any experience you may have in related fields, such as graphic design, web development, or project management. These skills and experiences can be valuable assets as you transition into a UX Design role.

Creating a Skills Inventory

Once you've evaluated your skills and experience, create a skills inventory to document your findings. This inventory can be a simple list, a spreadsheet, or even a visual representation, such as a mind map. Include the following information in your skills inventory:

- Skills and knowledge areas: List the specific skills and knowledge areas you've identified as strengths, as well as those you'd like to develop further.
- Current proficiency levels: For each skill or knowledge area, indicate your current level of proficiency using a simple rating scale, such as beginner, intermediate, or advanced.
- Goals for improvement: For each area where you'd like to improve, set a specific, measurable, and achievable goal that reflects your desired level of proficiency.
- Resources for growth: Identify the resources (books, courses, tutorials, etc.) that you plan to use to achieve your goals, and include a timeline for completing each resource.

Leveraging Your Existing Expertise

As you work to develop your UX Design skills, it's essential to recognize the value of your existing expertise. Here are some strategies for leveraging your current skills and experience to accelerate your transition into UX Design:

- Transferable skills: Identify any transferable skills from your previous work or educational experiences that can be applied to UX Design. For example, strong communication skills can be an asset when presenting design ideas to stakeholders, while project management experience can be beneficial when coordinating design projects and collaborating with team members.
- Related experience: If you have experience in fields like graphic design, web development, or marketing, consider how these skills can complement your UX Design expertise. For instance, a background in graphic design can enhance your visual design skills, while web development knowledge can help you better understand technical constraints and collaborate with developers.
- Learn from your past: Reflect on your previous work experiences and identify any lessons, insights, or best practices that can be applied to your new career in UX Design. This may include strategies for problem-solving, time management, or dealing with challenging situations.
- Network with professionals: Leverage your existing network to connect with UX Design professionals who can offer guidance, mentorship, or job leads. Attend industry events, join online communities, or participate in local meetups to expand your

network and gain valuable insights from others in the field.

Continually Reassess and Adjust Your Learning Plan

As you progress on your journey to becoming a UX Designer, it's important to regularly reassess your skills and experience to ensure you're on track to achieve your goals. Consider the following strategies for ongoing self-assessment:

- Periodic check-ins: Schedule periodic check-ins with yourself (every few months or at the end of a learning resource) to evaluate your progress, review your skills inventory, and adjust your learning plan as needed.
- Seek feedback: Solicit feedback from peers, mentors, or industry professionals on your work, and use this feedback to identify areas for growth and improvement.
- Reflect on your experiences: As you work on projects or complete learning resources, take the time to reflect on your experiences, considering what you've learned, what challenges you've faced, and how you've grown as a designer.

By continually assessing your skills and experience, you can ensure that your learning plan remains aligned with your goals and that you're making steady progress toward your desired career in UX Design.

In summary, taking stock of your current skills and experience is a critical step on your path to becoming a UX Designer. By understanding your strengths, identifying areas for improvement, and creating a targeted learning plan, you can effectively and efficiently develop the expertise needed to succeed in this exciting field.

leveraging transferable skills

As you transition into a career in UX Design, you might be surprised to discover that many of your existing skills can be applied in your new role. These transferable skills, which can be developed in various professional or educational contexts, can provide a valuable foundation for your UX Design journey. In this section, we'll explore the concept of transferable skills, discuss several key skills that are particularly relevant to UX Design, and provide strategies for leveraging your transferable skills to advance your career.

Understanding Transferable Skills

Transferable skills are abilities that can be used across different industries, job roles, and contexts. These skills are often developed through prior work experience, education, or personal interests and can be applied to a wide range of professional situations. Transferable skills are valuable because they can help you adapt to new roles and responsibilities, making you a more versatile and attractive candidate in the job market.

Key Transferable Skills for UX Design

While many transferable skills can be relevant to a career in UX Design, some are particularly important. Here are several key skills to consider:

- Communication: Effective communication is essential in UX Design, as you'll need to present your ideas, collaborate with team members, and gather feedback from users. If you have experience in public speaking, writing, or other communication-related roles, these skills will be valuable in your new career.
- Problem-solving: UX Designers are constantly faced with challenges, from identifying user pain points to developing innovative solutions that address

these issues. If you have a strong background in problem-solving, either through work experience or personal interests, this skill will serve you well in UX Design.

- Empathy: Understanding and empathizing with users is a critical component of UX Design. If you've worked in roles that involve interacting with customers, clients, or colleagues, you likely have developed empathy skills that can help you better understand the needs and experiences of your users.
- Analytical thinking: Analyzing data, identifying patterns, and drawing insights are important aspects of the UX Design process. If you have experience in fields like data analysis, market research, or even mathematics, you can leverage these analytical skills to inform your design decisions.
- Time management: UX Design projects often involve tight deadlines and competing priorities. If you've developed strong time management skills through previous work experience, these abilities can help you juggle multiple tasks and ensure your projects are completed on time.

Strategies for Leveraging Your Transferable Skills
Here are some strategies to help you leverage your transferable skills as you pursue a career in UX Design:

- Identify your strengths: Start by reflecting on your past experiences and identifying the transferable skills you've developed. Consider the roles you've held, the challenges you've faced, and the accomplishments you're most proud of, and think about the skills that contributed to your success.

- Connect the dots: Think about how your transferable skills can be applied in a UX Design context. For example, if you have strong problem-solving skills from working in engineering or consulting, consider how these abilities can help you identify user pain points and develop innovative design solutions.
- Showcase your skills: Highlight your transferable skills on your resume, portfolio, and during interviews. Provide concrete examples of how you've used these skills in the past and explain how they will be valuable in a UX Design role.
- Continue to develop your skills: Even if you have strong transferable skills, it's important to continue developing these abilities as you transition into UX Design. Seek opportunities to hone your skills, such as taking on challenging projects, attending workshops, or participating in online courses.

Embracing a Growth Mindset

As you work to leverage your transferable skills, it's important to embrace a growth mindset. This mindset involves believing that your abilities can be developed and improved over time through hard work, dedication, and learning. Adopting a growth mindset can help you remain open to new experiences, embrace challenges, and persevere in the face of setbacks.

Here are some strategies to cultivate a growth mindset as you leverage your transferable skills:

- Stay curious: Be open to learning new skills, exploring different UX Design techniques, and experimenting with new approaches. By staying curious, you'll be more likely to discover new ways to apply your existing skills in your new career.

- Embrace challenges: Don't shy away from difficult projects or tasks that push you outside of your comfort zone. Embracing challenges can help you grow and develop new skills that will make you a more effective UX Designer.
- Learn from feedback: Seek out feedback from peers, mentors, and colleagues, and use this input to identify areas for growth and improvement. Be open to constructive criticism and view it as an opportunity to learn and grow.
- Celebrate progress: Recognize and celebrate your progress as you develop your transferable skills and apply them to your UX Design work. Acknowledging your achievements can help you stay motivated and maintain a positive outlook on your career journey.

In conclusion, leveraging your transferable skills can be an effective strategy for transitioning into a career in UX Design. By identifying your existing strengths, connecting them to UX Design tasks, showcasing your skills, and embracing a growth mindset, you can build a strong foundation for success in this exciting field.

building a personal brand

In today's competitive job market, standing out as a UX Designer requires more than just a strong skill set and an impressive portfolio. Building a personal brand can help you differentiate yourself, showcase your unique value, and attract the attention of potential employers or clients. In this section, we'll discuss the importance of personal branding, offer strategies for developing a memorable brand, and provide tips for promoting your brand online and offline.

The Importance of Personal Branding

A personal brand is a unique blend of your skills, experiences, and personality that you showcase to the world. It's how you present yourself and the value you bring to the table. A strong personal brand can help you:

- Stand out from the competition: A well-crafted personal brand can differentiate you from other UX Designers and make you more memorable to potential employers or clients.
- Build credibility: A consistent and authentic personal brand can help establish you as an expert in your field, increasing your credibility and trustworthiness in the eyes of others.
- Attract opportunities: A compelling personal brand can act as a magnet for new job opportunities, freelance projects, or speaking engagements, as it showcases your unique talents and expertise.
- Expand your network: A personal brand can help you connect with like-minded professionals, opening up opportunities for collaboration, learning, and growth.

Developing Your Personal Brand

Creating a personal brand involves reflecting on your unique combination of skills, experiences, and values, and identifying the key elements that set you apart as a UX Designer. Here are some steps to help you develop your personal brand:

- Define your unique value proposition: Consider what makes you different from other UX Designers and identify your unique strengths and expertise. This could include your design philosophy, your approach to problem-solving, or your focus on specific industries or user groups.

- Identify your target audience: Think about who you want to reach with your personal brand, such as potential employers, clients, or collaborators. Understanding your target audience will help you tailor your brand messaging and ensure it resonates with the people who matter most to your career goals.
- Develop your brand messaging: Once you've defined your unique value proposition and identified your target audience, craft a clear and concise brand message that communicates your unique value. This message should be consistent across all your branding materials, including your resume, portfolio, and social media profiles.
- Choose your brand elements: Select visual elements that represent your personal brand, such as a logo, color palette, typography, and imagery. These elements should be consistent across all your branding materials and help convey your unique brand message.

Promoting Your Personal Brand

Once you've developed your personal brand, it's time to promote it and make it visible to your target audience. Here are some strategies for promoting your personal brand both online and offline:

- Optimize your online presence: Ensure your personal brand is reflected across all your online platforms, including your portfolio, LinkedIn profile, and social media accounts. Use consistent imagery, messaging, and tone to reinforce your brand identity.
- Engage with your target audience: Connect with potential employers, clients, and collaborators by

engaging with them on social media, attending industry events, or participating in online forums. Share your insights, ask questions, and offer value in your interactions to establish your credibility and showcase your expertise.

- Create and share valuable content: Demonstrate your thought leadership by creating and sharing content related to UX Design, such as blog posts, articles, or videos. This can help you showcase your expertise, engage with your target audience, and build your reputation in the industry.
- Network strategically: Attend industry events, conferences, and meetups to expand your network and connect with professionals who can help advance your career. Be intentional about building relationships and offering value to others in your interactions.
- Seek out speaking opportunities: Offer to speak at industry events, conferences, or webinars to share your expertise and showcase your personal brand. Speaking engagements can help you reach a wider audience and establish your credibility as a UX Designer.
- Collaborate with others: Partner with other professionals on projects, co-author articles, or participate in podcasts or panel discussions. Collaborating with others can help you expand your network, gain new insights, and increase your visibility within the UX Design community.
- Ask for recommendations and endorsements: Request recommendations from colleagues, clients, or mentors that highlight your skills, experiences, and unique value as a UX Designer. Display these recommendations on your LinkedIn profile or

portfolio to reinforce your personal brand and credibility.

Maintaining and Evolving Your Personal Brand

Developing a strong personal brand is an ongoing process that requires regular maintenance and evolution. As you grow in your career, your skills, experiences, and goals will change, and your personal brand should evolve to reflect these changes. Here are some tips for maintaining and evolving your personal brand:

- Continuously update your branding materials: Regularly review and update your resume, portfolio, and online profiles to ensure they accurately represent your current skills, experiences, and goals.
- Stay current with industry trends: Keep up to date with the latest developments in UX Design, and incorporate new skills, tools, or methodologies into your personal brand as needed.
- Seek out professional development opportunities: Attend workshops, conferences, or online courses to continue honing your skills and expanding your knowledge. This can help you stay relevant and competitive in the ever-evolving UX Design landscape.
- Reassess your brand messaging and target audience: Periodically revisit your unique value proposition and target audience to ensure your personal brand remains aligned with your career goals and aspirations.

Building a personal brand is an essential part of your journey as a UX Designer. By developing a strong, authentic, and memorable brand, you can stand out from the competition, attract opportunities, and establish yourself as an expert in your field.

networking in the ux design community

Networking is an essential aspect of any professional journey, and it is particularly crucial in the world of UX Design. Building connections within the UX Design community can lead to new opportunities, knowledge sharing, and collaboration, ultimately benefiting your career and personal growth. In this section, we'll explore the importance of networking, offer tips for effective networking, and provide suggestions for finding networking opportunities within the UX Design community.

The Importance of Networking

Networking can yield numerous benefits for UX Designers, such as:

- Access to job opportunities: Many job opportunities are not advertised publicly, and networking can help you tap into this hidden job market. Additionally, having connections within the industry can lead to job referrals, increasing your chances of securing interviews and job offers.
- Knowledge sharing: Networking with other UX Designers can provide valuable insights into industry trends, best practices, and new tools and techniques. This knowledge sharing can help you stay current and improve your skills.
- Collaboration and partnerships: Building connections with other UX Designers can lead to collaboration on projects or even partnerships for your freelance work or design agency.
- Support and mentorship: Connecting with experienced UX Designers can provide you with

guidance, mentorship, and support as you navigate your career.

- Increased visibility: Actively participating in the UX Design community can raise your profile, showcase your expertise, and make you more visible to potential employers or clients.

Tips for Effective Networking

Networking can feel daunting, but with the right approach, you can make meaningful connections that benefit your career. Here are some tips for effective networking:

- Be genuine: Approach networking with the intention of building authentic relationships, rather than merely collecting contacts. Show genuine interest in others and their work, and aim to offer value in your interactions.
- Listen more than you talk: When networking, make an effort to listen actively and attentively to others. This will help you understand their needs, interests, and experiences, and allow you to tailor your conversations accordingly.
- Focus on quality over quantity: It's more valuable to have a few meaningful connections than a large number of superficial ones. Invest time and effort into nurturing relationships with people who share your interests and values, and with whom you can build a mutual support system.
- Be prepared with an elevator pitch: Develop a brief, compelling introduction that succinctly explains who you are, what you do, and what sets you apart as a UX Designer. This can help you make a strong first impression during networking events or conversations.

- Follow up: After meeting someone new, make an effort to follow up with a personalized message, expressing your gratitude for the conversation and expressing interest in staying connected. This can help you build lasting relationships and ensure you remain top of mind for future opportunities.

Finding Networking Opportunities in the UX Design Community

There are numerous networking opportunities within the UX Design community, both online and offline. Here are some suggestions for finding and engaging with networking opportunities:

- Local meetups and events: Attend local UX Design meetups, workshops, or events to connect with other professionals in your area. Look for event listings on websites like Meetup.com or through local UX Design organizations.
- Conferences: Attend national or international UX Design conferences to expand your network and learn from industry experts. Some popular UX Design conferences include UXPA, Interaction, and UX Week.
- Online forums and communities: Join UX Design-focused online forums or communities, such as UX Stack Exchange, Designer Hangout, or UX Mastery, to engage in discussions, ask questions, and share your knowledge with other professionals.
- Social media: Follow and engage with UX Designers and industry influencers on social media platforms like Twitter and LinkedIn. Participate in UX Design-related Twitter chats or LinkedIn groups to connect with like-minded professionals.

Professional associations: Join UX Design professional associations, such as the User Experience Professionals Association (UXPA) or Interaction Design Association (IxDA). These organizations offer networking events, resources, and opportunities to connect with other professionals in the field.

- Alumni networks: Connect with your college or university's alumni network, as these groups often host networking events and can provide valuable connections within the UX Design community.
- Volunteering and mentorship: Offer to volunteer or mentor at UX Design workshops, bootcamps, or local schools. This can help you build connections while also giving back to the community and supporting the growth of future UX Designers.
- Networking with non-UX professionals: Expand your network beyond the UX Design community by attending networking events or joining professional organizations in related fields, such as web development, graphic design, or marketing. This can help you build a diverse network and open up opportunities for collaboration.

Nurturing Your Network

Building your network is just the first step; nurturing your relationships is equally important. Here are some tips for maintaining and strengthening your connections within the UX Design community:

- Stay in touch: Regularly reach out to your contacts to check in, share updates, or offer support. This can help you maintain strong relationships and keep your network engaged.
- Share resources and opportunities: Be generous with your knowledge, resources, and opportunities,

and share them with your network. This can help you build trust and goodwill and establish yourself as a valuable member of the UX Design community.

- Celebrate others' successes: Congratulate your connections on their achievements, such as promotions, awards, or new projects. This can help you strengthen your relationships and demonstrate your genuine interest in their success.
- Be a connector: Introduce your contacts to one another when you see potential for collaboration or mutual benefit. This can help you facilitate new connections within the community and demonstrate your commitment to supporting others.

Networking is an essential aspect of a successful career in UX Design. By engaging with the UX Design community, you can create valuable connections, access new opportunities, and enhance your professional growth. Approach networking with a genuine, authentic mindset, and focus on building relationships that offer mutual support and value. With a strong network, you'll be well-positioned to thrive in the dynamic world of UX Design.

gaining practical experience through internships, freelancing, and side projects

As you embark on your journey to becoming a UX Designer, one of the most crucial aspects of your professional development is gaining practical experience. In addition to formal education and self-study, real-world experience will help you refine your skills, build your portfolio, and increase your employability. In this section, we'll discuss the value of internships, freelancing, and side projects in building your UX

Design expertise and offer tips for securing and succeeding in these opportunities.

Internships

Internships can be an invaluable stepping stone for aspiring UX Designers, providing hands-on experience and an introduction to the professional world of UX. Here's why internships are important and how to make the most of them:

- Learning from experienced professionals: Internships offer the opportunity to work alongside and learn from experienced UX Designers. This mentorship can help you hone your skills and gain practical insights into the industry.
- Building your portfolio: As an intern, you'll work on real-world projects, which can be showcased in your portfolio as evidence of your skills and experience.
- Networking: Internships can help you build connections within the UX Design community, which can lead to future job opportunities or collaborations.
- Assessing your fit for the industry: Internships allow you to experience the day-to-day work of a UX Designer, helping you evaluate whether it's the right career path for you.

To secure a UX Design internship, consider the following steps:

- Research potential companies and opportunities: Identify organizations that align with your values and interests, and search for UX Design internship openings on their websites or job boards.

- Tailor your application: Customize your resume and cover letter to highlight your relevant skills, experiences, and passion for UX Design.
- Leverage your network: Reach out to connections in the industry to inquire about potential internship opportunities or to ask for referrals.

Freelancing

Freelancing can be a great way to build your UX Design experience while offering flexibility and the opportunity to work on diverse projects. Here's how freelancing can benefit your career and tips for getting started:

- Diversifying your experience: As a freelancer, you'll work with a range of clients and projects, which can help you develop a versatile skill set and expand your portfolio.
- Building your personal brand: Freelancing allows you to establish yourself as an independent UX Designer, helping you build your reputation and personal brand within the industry.
- Earning income: Freelancing can provide a source of income while you continue to learn and grow in your UX Design career.

To get started as a freelance UX Designer, consider these tips:

- Create a professional website: Develop a website showcasing your portfolio, services, and contact information. This will serve as your online business card and help potential clients find you.
- Market your services: Use social media, online forums, and networking events to promote your

freelance UX Design services and connect with potential clients.

- Build a client base: Start by offering your services to friends, family, or local businesses to gain initial experience and build a client base.

Side Projects

Side projects can be another effective way to gain practical UX Design experience while exploring your interests and passions. Here's how side projects can benefit your career and some ideas for getting started:

- Developing new skills: Side projects allow you to experiment with new techniques, tools, or approaches, helping you expand your UX Design skill set.
- Showcasing your initiative: Including side projects in your portfolio demonstrates your passion for UX Design and your drive to learn and grow outside of formal work settings.
- Discovering your niche: Side projects can help you identify specific areas of UX Design that interest you, which can inform your career choices and specialization.

To get started with side projects, consider these ideas:

- Redesign an existing app or website: Choose an app or website that you feel could benefit from a UX overhaul, and work on improving its user experience. This can help you develop your problem-solving and design skills, as well as showcase your ability to identify areas for improvement.

arah Michaels

- Collaborate with others: Partner with friends or colleagues on a UX Design project, or join a local hackathon or design challenge. Collaborating with others can help you learn from their perspectives, build your teamwork skills, and expand your network.
- Create a passion project: Identify a cause or interest that you're passionate about and develop a UX Design project around it. This could be designing an app to support a nonprofit organization, creating a website to promote sustainability, or developing a digital tool to improve mental health.

Balancing Experience-building Opportunities

As you gain practical experience through internships, free-lancing, and side projects, it's essential to strike a balance between these opportunities and your other commitments, such as formal education, self-study, and networking. Here are some tips for managing your time and energy effectively:

- Prioritize your goals: Set clear goals for your UX Design career and prioritize your efforts accordingly. For example, if your primary objective is to build your portfolio, focus on projects that will showcase your skills and creativity.
- Set boundaries: Establish boundaries to prevent burnout and ensure that you have enough time and energy for all aspects of your professional development. This might include setting specific work hours, limiting the number of projects you take on, or dedicating specific days for self-study or networking.
- Be strategic with your opportunities: Choose internships, freelancing projects, and side projects that align with your career goals and interests. This

will help you make the most of your time and ensure that your efforts are contributing to your overall professional growth.

As you advance on your path to becoming a UX Designer, gaining practical experience through internships, freelancing, and side projects will play a vital role in your professional development. These opportunities will help you refine your skills, build your portfolio, and establish a strong foundation for a successful career in UX Design. Embrace the challenges, learn from your experiences, and enjoy the journey as you grow and evolve as a UX Designer.

4 /
building a standout portfolio

importance of a strong portfolio

A JOURNEY into the world of UX Design would be incomplete without discussing the significance of a strong portfolio. As an aspiring UX Designer, your portfolio is your calling card, showcasing your skills, creativity, and experience to potential employers and clients. In this section, we'll delve into the importance of having a robust portfolio, tips for creating an effective one, and how to present your work to stand out in a competitive market.

Why a Strong Portfolio Matters

Having a well-crafted portfolio is essential for several reasons:

- Demonstrating your skills: Your portfolio is a tangible representation of your UX Design abilities. It allows potential employers and clients to see the depth and breadth of your skills, as well as your attention to detail and design sensibilities.
- Showcasing your experience: Your portfolio should include examples of real-world projects that you've worked on, whether through internships,

freelancing, or side projects. This demonstrates your ability to apply your skills in practical situations and adapt to different client needs.

- Telling your story: A strong portfolio tells the story of your growth as a UX Designer, showcasing your unique perspective, passions, and journey in the field. This personal narrative can help you stand out from the competition and make a memorable impression on potential employers and clients.
- Building your personal brand: Your portfolio is an essential component of your personal brand, reflecting your professional identity and the value you bring to UX Design projects. A well-designed portfolio can help you establish credibility and authority in the industry.

Tips for Creating an Effective Portfolio

To create a strong and compelling portfolio, consider the following tips:

- Be selective: Choose a diverse selection of your best work that demonstrates your skills and experience. Include projects that highlight your strengths, showcase your creativity, and represent your unique perspective on UX Design.
- Provide context: For each project, provide a brief description that explains the problem you were solving, your role, the tools and techniques used, and the outcomes achieved. This context helps potential employers and clients understand the rationale behind your design decisions and the value you bring to a project.
- Show your process: Your portfolio should not only showcase the final outcome of your projects but also highlight your design process. Include

sketches, wireframes, user flows, and other artifacts that demonstrate your approach to problem-solving and the evolution of your design ideas.

- Keep it up to date: Regularly update your portfolio with new projects and accomplishments, ensuring that it remains a current and accurate representation of your skills and experience.

Presenting Your Portfolio

How you present your portfolio can significantly impact how potential employers and clients perceive your work. Here are some tips for presenting your portfolio effectively:

- Create a professional website: Develop a clean, user-friendly website that showcases your portfolio, along with your resume, contact information, and any relevant certifications or awards. Ensure that your website is easy to navigate, visually appealing, and optimized for both desktop and mobile devices.
- Use high-quality visuals: Include high-resolution images, screenshots, or videos of your work, ensuring that your projects are presented clearly and professionally. Consider using tools like mockups or interactive prototypes to provide a more immersive experience for visitors.
- Organize your content: Organize your projects in a logical and cohesive manner, grouping similar projects together or presenting them in chronological order. This organization will help potential employers and clients quickly find the information they're looking for and get a sense of your experience and skills.
- Optimize for search engines: Use search engine optimization (SEO) techniques to improve the

visibility of your portfolio website on search engine results pages. This will increase the likelihood of potential employers and clients discovering your work.

A strong portfolio is a vital asset for any aspiring UX Designer, showcasing your skills, experience, and unique perspective on UX Design. By investing time and effort into creating a compelling and professional portfolio, you can make a lasting impression on potential employers and clients, setting the stage for a successful career in the field.

Utilizing Feedback and Iteration

As a UX Designer, you understand the importance of feedback and iteration in the design process. Don't be afraid to apply these principles to your portfolio as well. Seek feedback from peers, mentors, and professionals in the industry. Use their insights to refine your portfolio, making it more effective and impactful.

- Participate in portfolio reviews: Many design communities and organizations host portfolio review events, providing an opportunity for you to receive constructive feedback on your work. Attend these events to gain valuable insights and make connections with other professionals in the industry.
- Share your work online: Use social media platforms and design forums to share your portfolio with a broader audience. This can help you gather feedback from diverse perspectives and potentially attract the attention of potential employers and clients.
- Be open to constructive criticism: When receiving feedback, be open to constructive criticism and embrace the opportunity to learn and grow. Use the

insights you gain to iterate on your portfolio and improve its overall quality.

Standing Out from the Competition

In a competitive job market, it's essential to make your portfolio stand out from the crowd. Here are some strategies to help you differentiate yourself:

- Develop a unique visual style: Create a consistent visual identity across your portfolio that reflects your personal brand and design sensibilities. This can help you establish a memorable presence and showcase your creativity.
- Highlight your unique strengths: Emphasize the skills, experiences, and interests that set you apart from other UX Designers. This could include specialized training, proficiency in specific design tools, or a passion for a particular industry or cause.
- Showcase real-world impact: Whenever possible, include metrics or testimonials that demonstrate the real-world impact of your work. This can help potential employers and clients understand the value you bring to UX Design projects.
- Tell compelling stories: Use storytelling techniques to bring your projects to life, engaging your audience and helping them understand the context, challenges, and outcomes of your work.

A strong portfolio is an essential component of your UX Design career journey. By showcasing your skills, experience, and unique perspective, you can make a lasting impression on potential employers and clients, and set the stage for a fulfilling and successful career in the field. Remember to continually refine and update your portfolio, embrace feedback and iteration, and strive to differentiate yourself in a competitive market. Your hard work and dedication will undoubtedly pay off as you establish yourself as a skilled and sought-after UX Designer.

showcase your design process

As you embark on your journey to become a successful UX Designer, it's essential to understand the importance of showcasing your design process in your portfolio. A well-documented design process not only illustrates your skills and expertise but also provides insight into how you approach problem-solving, collaboration, and the various stages of a design project. In this section, we'll discuss the importance of showcasing your design process, the key components to include, and how to present your process in a clear, engaging, and professional manner.

The Importance of Showcasing Your Design Process

The design process is at the heart of UX Design. By presenting a detailed account of your design journey for each project in your portfolio, you can effectively communicate your skills, thought process, and overall approach to potential employers and clients. Showcasing your design process:

- Demonstrates your problem-solving abilities: Employers and clients are interested in how you approach design challenges and the methods you use to find creative solutions. Your design process allows them to see your problem-solving skills in action.
- Highlights your attention to detail: Presenting a well-documented design process shows that you pay attention to detail, a critical trait for a successful UX Designer.

- Showcases your ability to work collaboratively: UX Design is often a collaborative effort involving various stakeholders, such as developers, product managers, and marketing teams. By illustrating how you collaborate with others during the design process, you can showcase your ability to work effectively in a team environment.

Key Components of Your Design Process

While each designer's process may differ slightly, there are some key components that you should consider including in your portfolio:

- Research: Explain the initial research phase of your project, including user interviews, surveys, market analysis, and competitor analysis. Be sure to highlight the insights you gained from your research and how they informed your design decisions.
- Persona development: Showcase the user personas you created based on your research. Explain how these personas helped guide your design choices and ensured that you kept the end-user in mind throughout the project.
- Information architecture and user flows: Describe the process of organizing and structuring the content and features of the product, as well as how you developed user flows to map out the user's journey through the product.
- Wireframing and prototyping: Discuss your approach to creating low-fidelity wireframes and high-fidelity prototypes, and how these iterative steps allowed you to refine your design based on user feedback and testing.

- User testing: Explain your user testing methods, such as usability testing, A/B testing, or remote testing, and how the feedback you received helped you iterate on your design.
- Final design and implementation: Present the final design of your project, including any necessary documentation for developers or other stakeholders. Discuss any challenges or lessons learned during the implementation phase.

Presenting Your Design Process in a Clear and Engaging Manner

When showcasing your design process, it's crucial to present the information in a clear, engaging, and visually appealing manner. Consider the following tips:

- Use visuals to support your narrative: Incorporate relevant images, such as sketches, wireframes, and screenshots, to help illustrate your design process. Visuals can make your process more engaging and easier to understand.
- Organize your content logically: Structure your design process in a logical, chronological order, making it easy for viewers to follow along. Use clear headings and subheadings to break up your content and guide readers through your narrative.
- Be concise and focused: While it's important to provide a thorough account of your design process, avoid overwhelming your audience with too much detail. Keep your descriptions concise and focused, highlighting only the most relevant and impactful aspects of your process.
- Use storytelling techniques: Engage your audience by telling a compelling story about your design process. Share your challenges, successes, and

learnings in a way that keeps your audience interested and invested in your journey.

- Include context and rationale: When presenting your design decisions, always provide context and explain the rationale behind them. This allows your audience to understand the reasoning behind your choices and demonstrates that your decisions were informed and purposeful.
- Showcase the evolution of your design: Highlight the progression of your design from initial concepts to final implementation, emphasizing the iterative nature of the design process. This will help your audience appreciate the evolution and refinement of your work.

Tailoring Your Design Process Presentation to Your Audience

When showcasing your design process, it's essential to tailor your presentation to your specific audience. Consider the following tips to ensure that your design process resonates with your target audience:

- Research your audience: Understand the needs, expectations, and preferences of your target audience. This will help you craft a design process presentation that addresses their concerns and interests.
- Focus on relevant projects: Choose projects that are most relevant to your audience and their industry. This will help demonstrate your expertise in their specific domain and increase the likelihood of engaging their interest.
- Highlight the skills and techniques that matter most: Emphasize the skills, techniques, and tools that are most relevant and important to your

audience. This will help showcase your expertise in the areas that matter most to them.

- Adapt your tone and language: Adjust your tone and language to match the preferences of your audience. For example, if you're presenting to a more technical audience, you may want to use more technical language and focus on the details of your process. On the other hand, if your audience is more focused on the business side, you may want to emphasize the impact of your design on user satisfaction and the bottom line.

Showcasing your design process in your portfolio is a crucial aspect of demonstrating your skills, expertise, and approach to UX Design. By presenting a clear, engaging, and professional account of your design journey, you can effectively communicate your value to potential employers and clients, setting yourself apart in the competitive world of UX Design.

capturing your success: documenting case studies in ux design

This is an essential part of your UX design portfolio, as case studies are the backbone of showcasing your skills, experience, and achievements. In this section, we will explore the importance of case studies, what they should include, and how to create compelling, engaging narratives around your design projects.

Why Case Studies Are Important

Case studies are important for several reasons. They allow you to:

- Demonstrate your skills and expertise: A well-documented case study shows your ability to apply

UX design principles to real-world projects, illustrating your skills and expertise in action.

- Share your design process: By showcasing the steps you took to address a design challenge, you can demonstrate your systematic approach, critical thinking, and problem-solving skills.
- Provide evidence of your impact: Case studies offer tangible examples of how your designs have improved user experiences, driven business results, or solved critical issues, which adds credibility to your work.
- Connect with your audience: A well-written case study tells a story that helps your audience understand and appreciate the value of your work, which can foster a deeper connection with potential clients or employers.

Key Components of a Case Study

A successful case study should include the following components:

- Project overview: Begin with a brief introduction to the project, its context, and its goals. This sets the stage for the rest of the case study.
- Problem statement: Clearly articulate the problem or challenge you were trying to solve. This helps your audience understand the need for your design intervention.
- User research and insights: Describe any user research you conducted, such as interviews, surveys, or usability tests. Share the key insights you gained from this research and explain how they informed your design decisions.
- Design process and iterations: Detail the steps you took to address the problem, from initial concepts

and wireframes to prototypes and final designs. Emphasize the iterative nature of your design process and explain how you refined your ideas based on user feedback, testing, and other considerations.

- Results and impact: Share the outcomes of your design work, such as improvements in user satisfaction, increased conversions, or other relevant metrics. Be sure to connect these results to the problem statement and show how your design contributed to the project's success.
- Reflections and lessons learned: Conclude your case study with a reflection on what you learned from the project, any challenges you faced, and how you would approach similar projects in the future.

Crafting a Compelling Narrative

A great case study tells a story that engages your audience and keeps them interested in your work. Here are some tips for crafting a compelling narrative around your design projects:

- Use a clear and logical structure: Organize your case study in a way that makes it easy for your audience to follow, using headings and subheadings to guide them through each section.
- Tell a story: Frame your case study as a narrative, with a beginning, middle, and end. Start by setting the scene and introducing the problem, then guide your audience through your design process and its iterations, and finally, reveal the results and impact of your work.
- Be concise and focused: Keep your case study to the point, focusing on the most important aspects of

your project. Avoid including too many details that might distract or confuse your audience.

- Use visuals to support your narrative: Include relevant images, such as wireframes, mockups, and screenshots, to help your audience visualize your design process and its outcomes. Visuals can be a powerful way to communicate your ideas and make your case study more engaging.
- Maintain a consistent tone and voice: Write your case study in a friendly, conversational tone that is consistent with the rest of your portfolio. This will help your audience connect with your work and understand your perspective as a designer.

Tailoring Case Studies for Different Audiences

Keep in mind that different audiences may be interested in different aspects of your work. For example, potential clients may be more focused on the business impact of your designs, while fellow designers may be more interested in your creative process and design rationale. Consider tailoring your case studies to address the specific needs and interests of your target audience:

- Highlight relevant skills and expertise: Emphasize the aspects of your work that are most relevant to your audience's needs. For example, if you are targeting clients in a specific industry, focus on case studies that demonstrate your experience and success in that sector.
- Address common pain points: Identify the challenges and pain points that are most relevant to your audience, and show how your design work has helped to address these issues. This can help to establish your credibility and demonstrate the value of your services.

- Use language that resonates with your audience: Speak the same language as your target audience, using terms and concepts that they are likely to be familiar with. This will help to establish a rapport and make your case studies more relatable and accessible.

Updating and Refining Your Case Studies

As your career progresses and your portfolio grows, it's important to regularly update and refine your case studies to reflect your latest work and achievements. Here are some tips for keeping your case studies fresh and relevant:

- Update your results and impact: As new data becomes available, be sure to update the results and impact of your designs to reflect the latest information. This will help to keep your case studies current and demonstrate the ongoing value of your work.
- Incorporate new projects: As you complete new projects, consider adding them to your portfolio as new case studies. This will help to showcase the breadth and depth of your experience and keep your portfolio up to date.
- Refine your storytelling: As you gain more experience as a designer, you may find new and more effective ways to tell the story of your design projects. Look for opportunities to refine your storytelling and make your case studies even more engaging and compelling.
- Seek feedback from others: Ask for feedback from clients, colleagues, and mentors on your case studies. This can help you identify areas for improvement and uncover new perspectives that you may not have considered.

Documenting case studies is a crucial aspect of show-casing your UX design skills and experience. A well-crafted case study tells the story of your design projects, demon-strates your expertise, and provides tangible evidence of your impact. By following the tips and guidelines outlined in this section, you can create compelling, engaging case studies that resonate with your target audience and set you apart from the competition..

tips for portfolio presentation

The presentation of your UX design portfolio can make or break your chances of landing that dream job or scoring a high-profile client. In this section, we'll explore some essential tips for creating a polished, professional, and engaging port-folio presentation that will help you stand out from the competition and showcase your design expertise.

Choose the Right Platform

First things first, you'll need to decide on the platform you'll use to host and present your portfolio. There are numerous options available, from dedicated portfolio websites like Dribbble and Behance to creating your own custom website using a platform like WordPress or Webflow. Consider the following factors when selecting your platform:

- Flexibility: Choose a platform that allows you to customize the look and feel of your portfolio, so you can create a unique and memorable online presence.
- Ease of use: Opt for a platform that is easy to update and maintain, ensuring that you can quickly add new projects and make changes as needed.
- Integration with other services: Select a platform that integrates with other services, like LinkedIn or

social media platforms, to maximize your exposure and reach a wider audience.

Prioritize Quality Over Quantity

When it comes to portfolio presentation, less is often more. It's better to showcase a few outstanding projects that demonstrate your design skills and expertise than to overwhelm your audience with a large volume of mediocre work. Focus on including projects that:

- Demonstrate your range and versatility as a designer
- Showcase your problem-solving abilities and design thinking
- Highlight your proficiency with different tools and technologies
- Feature compelling case studies, as discussed in the previous section

Optimize for Mobile Devices

In today's digital landscape, a large percentage of your audience will likely access your portfolio on mobile devices. Ensure that your portfolio is responsive and optimized for viewing on a variety of screen sizes and devices. Test your portfolio on multiple devices and browsers to ensure a seamless user experience, and make any necessary adjustments to improve performance and usability.

Use High-Quality Images and Visuals

Visuals are an integral part of any design portfolio, and the quality of your images can have a significant impact on the overall impression you make. Invest in high-quality images and visuals for your portfolio, and consider the following tips:

- Use large, high-resolution images that showcase the details of your work
- Opt for consistent image sizes and aspect ratios to create a cohesive visual experience
- Choose images that highlight key aspects of your design process, from initial sketches and wireframes to final mockups and prototypes

Organize Your Projects Strategically

The organization and structure of your portfolio can greatly influence how your work is perceived. Arrange your projects strategically to create a smooth, engaging flow that guides your audience through your design journey:

- Lead with your strongest work: Start your portfolio with your most impressive projects to immediately capture your audience's attention.
- Group similar projects: Organize projects with similar themes or industries together to help demonstrate your expertise in specific areas.
- Use clear navigation: Ensure that your portfolio is easy to navigate, with intuitive menus, headings, and links that make it simple for users to explore your work.

Provide Context and Insight

While your designs may speak for themselves, it's essential to provide context and insight into your work. Accompany each project with a brief description that covers:

- The project's goals and objectives
- The challenges and constraints you faced
- Your design process and approach
- The results and impact of your work

This information will help your audience understand your thought process, decision-making, and the value you bring as a UX designer.

Proofread and Edit

Finally, take the time to proofread and edit your portfolio thoroughly. Typos, grammatical errors, and inconsistencies can detract from the overall professionalism of your presentation, leaving a negative impression on potential employers or clients. Consider the following tips for proofreading and editing:

- Check for spelling and grammar errors: Use a tool like Grammarly or enlist a friend to review your portfolio for any mistakes you may have missed.
- Ensure consistency: Make sure your formatting, typography, and style choices are consistent throughout your portfolio. This will help create a polished and cohesive presentation.
- Refine your copy: Keep your descriptions and explanations clear, concise, and engaging. Eliminate any unnecessary jargon or buzzwords, and focus on effectively communicating the key aspects of your work.

Solicit Feedback

Before launching your portfolio, it's a good idea to solicit feedback from trusted peers, mentors, or colleagues. Their insights can help you identify areas for improvement, uncover any overlooked errors, and ensure that your portfolio presents your work in the best possible light. Be open to constructive criticism and use the feedback you receive to refine and enhance your presentation.

Promote Your Portfolio

Once you've crafted a stunning portfolio presentation, it's time to share it with the world. Promote your portfolio through various channels to increase your visibility and attract potential employers or clients:

- Share your portfolio on social media platforms like LinkedIn, Twitter, and Instagram
- Include a link to your portfolio in your email signature and on your resume
- Attend industry events and conferences, and network with other professionals who can help spread the word about your work

Keep Your Portfolio Updated

A strong portfolio is an evolving showcase of your skills and accomplishments. Regularly update your portfolio with new projects, case studies, and experiences to demonstrate your continued growth as a UX designer. This not only keeps your portfolio fresh and engaging but also helps to convey your commitment to staying current in the ever-changing world of UX design.

In summary, an exceptional portfolio presentation can greatly enhance your prospects as a UX designer. By selecting the right platform, prioritizing quality over quantity, optimizing for mobile devices, using high-quality images, organizing your projects strategically, providing context, proofreading and editing, soliciting feedback, promoting your portfolio, and keeping it updated, you'll create a compelling showcase of your design expertise that will set you apart from the competition. Remember, your portfolio is a reflection of your unique style, approach, and capabilities—make sure it leaves a lasting impression.

online portfolio platforms and tools

In the world of UX design, your portfolio is your ticket to showcasing your skills, creativity, and experience to potential employers and clients. A well-crafted online portfolio can help you stand out from the crowd and land your dream job or project. With so many online portfolio platforms and tools available, it can be challenging to decide which one is right for you. In this section, we'll explore the key features and benefits of popular online portfolio platforms and tools to help you make an informed decision.

Behance

Owned by Adobe, Behance is a popular platform for creative professionals to showcase their work in various fields, including UX design, graphic design, photography, and illustration. With its clean and user-friendly interface, Behance allows you to create a visually appealing portfolio that highlights your best projects and case studies.

Key features:

- Integration with Adobe Creative Cloud
- Customizable project layouts
- Ability to create mood boards and collections
- Job board and networking opportunities

Dribbble

Dribbble is a well-known platform for designers to share their work, find inspiration, and connect with a global community of creative professionals. While it started as an invite-only platform, Dribbble now allows anyone to sign up and showcase their portfolio.

Key features:

- Simple and clean user interface
- Design feedback and collaboration tools
- Job board and freelance project opportunities
- Pro membership option for additional features and benefits

Adobe Portfolio

Adobe Portfolio is a powerful and easy-to-use website builder specifically designed for creative professionals. With its seamless integration with Adobe Creative Cloud, it allows you to quickly and effortlessly create a polished online portfolio.

Key features:

- Customizable templates and layouts
- Integration with Adobe Creative Cloud
- Responsive design for optimal viewing on various devices
- Included with Adobe Creative Cloud subscription

1. Squarespace

Squarespace is a popular website builder known for its beautiful templates and user-friendly interface. While not specifically designed for UX designers, Squarespace offers a range of customizable templates that can be tailored to showcase your design work.

Key features:

- Elegant and responsive templates
- Custom domain and hosting options
- E-commerce integration for selling products or services
- Built-in analytics and SEO tools

Wix

Wix is a versatile website builder with a wide array of templates and customization options. Its drag-and-drop editor makes it easy for anyone to create a professional-looking portfolio without any coding knowledge.

Key features:

- Drag-and-drop website builder
- Large selection of customizable templates
- App market with various add-ons and integrations
- Free and premium plans available

Webflow

Webflow is a powerful web design tool that combines the ease of a visual editor with the flexibility of custom code. While it has a steeper learning curve than some other platforms, Webflow offers advanced design capabilities and the ability to create unique, responsive portfolios.

Key features:

- Visual editor with custom code capabilities
- Responsive design and CSS grid support
- Built-in hosting and SSL certification
- Client billing and e-commerce features

Cargo

Cargo is a portfolio platform tailored specifically for creative professionals. It offers a curated selection of templates and allows you to create a visually appealing online presence with minimal effort.

Key features:

- Curated templates designed for creative portfolios
- Customizable typography and layout options
- Password protection for private projects
- Integrated analytics and SEO tools

As you consider the various online portfolio platforms and tools, keep in mind the following factors:

- Your level of technical expertise: Some platforms are more beginner-friendly, while others cater to users with more advanced coding knowledge.
- Customization options: Look for a platform that offers a range of templates and customization features to create a portfolio that reflects your unique style and brand.
- Cost: Determine your budget and compare the pricing plans of different platforms. Some offer free plans with basic features, while others require a subscription or one-time fee for more advanced options.
- Integration with other tools: If you already use certain tools, like Adobe Creative Cloud, consider platforms that offer seamless integration for a more streamlined workflow.
- Community and networking opportunities: Some platforms come with built-in networking features, job boards, and design communities that can help you connect with other professionals and find new opportunities.

Once you've chosen a platform that suits your needs, keep these tips in mind for creating a compelling online portfolio:

1. Prioritize quality over quantity: Focus on showcasing your best work rather than including every project you've ever completed. A carefully curated selection of projects will make a stronger impression on potential clients or employers.
2. Use high-quality images and visuals: Ensure that your portfolio images are crisp, clear, and visually appealing. High-quality visuals will help convey your attention to detail and professionalism.

3. Make it easy to navigate: Organize your portfolio in a way that's easy for visitors to navigate and understand. Consider using categories, tags, or filters to help users find relevant projects quickly.

4. Include detailed project descriptions: For each project, provide a brief overview, your role, the tools and technologies used, and any challenges or key learnings. This will help visitors understand the context and scope of your work.

5. Optimize for mobile devices: With more and more people accessing the web via smartphones and tablets, it's essential to ensure your portfolio looks great and functions smoothly on all devices.

6. Update your portfolio regularly: As you complete new projects or acquire new skills, be sure to update your portfolio to reflect your most recent work and accomplishments.

By selecting the right online portfolio platform and following these tips, you'll be well on your way to creating a stunning, effective portfolio that showcases your unique talents and helps you stand out in the competitive world of UX design.

5 /
preparing for ux design job interviews

understanding the ux design job market

AS YOU EMBARK on your journey to become a UX designer, it's crucial to understand the job market you're entering. Knowing the ins and outs of the UX design job market can help you make informed decisions about your career trajectory and ensure you're positioning yourself as a competitive candidate.

In this section, we'll explore various aspects of the UX design job market, including industry growth, types of companies hiring UX designers, roles and responsibilities, and common job titles. We'll also touch on the importance of soft skills and how to keep up with evolving industry trends.

Industry growth

The demand for UX designers has skyrocketed in recent years, with companies of all sizes recognizing the value of creating user-friendly products and services. According to the Bureau of Labor Statistics, employment of web developers and digital designers, including UX designers, is projected to grow significantly faster than the average for all occupations over the next decade.

This growth can be attributed to several factors, such as

the increased use of mobile devices, the rise of e-commerce, and the growing emphasis on user experience as a key differentiator in competitive markets. As a result, UX design is an attractive field with ample job opportunities for aspiring designers.

Types of companies hiring UX designers

UX designers can find employment opportunities in a wide range of industries and company sizes. Some common types of companies that hire UX designers include:

- Tech startups: Startups focused on developing new digital products or services often require UX designers to create intuitive and engaging user experiences from the ground up.
- Large corporations: Many established companies have in-house UX design teams responsible for maintaining and improving existing products or developing new ones.
- Design agencies: UX designers working at design agencies typically collaborate with various clients to create user experiences for different products and services.
- Freelance and consulting: Some UX designers choose to work independently, offering their services on a project-by-project basis or as consultants for companies in need of UX expertise.

Roles and responsibilities

While the specific responsibilities of a UX designer may vary depending on the company and project, some common tasks include:

- Conducting user research to understand user needs, behaviors, and motivations

- Creating user personas and scenarios to guide design decisions
- Developing information architecture, such as site maps and navigation systems
- Designing wireframes, mockups, and prototypes to communicate design concepts
- Conducting usability testing and iterating on designs based on user feedback
- Collaborating with other designers, developers, and stakeholders to ensure a cohesive user experience

Common job titles

In the UX design field, job titles can vary widely and may not always include the term "UX designer." Some common job titles related to UX design include:

- User Experience Designer
- Interaction Designer
- User Interface (UI) Designer
- Product Designer
- User Researcher
- Information Architect

It's important to read job descriptions carefully, as the responsibilities associated with these titles can differ from one company to another. Additionally, some roles may combine elements of UX and UI design, while others focus primarily on one aspect.

The importance of soft skills

While technical skills and design expertise are crucial for a successful career in UX design, soft skills can be just as important. Employers often value UX designers who possess strong communication, teamwork, and problem-solving abilities.

Other desirable soft skills include empathy, adaptability, and a user-centered mindset.

Developing your soft skills can not only make you a more effective UX designer but also set you apart from other candidates in the job market.

Keeping up with industry trends

As technology and user needs continue to evolve, so too does the field of UX design. To stay competitive in the job market, it's essential to stay informed about emerging trends, best practices, and new tools and technologies. You can keep up with industry developments by attending conferences, participating in online forums and communities, reading industry publications, and following thought leaders on social media. Staying abreast of new developments can help you anticipate and adapt to changes in the job market and ensure your skills remain relevant.

Preparing for job interviews

Acing a UX design job interview often requires a mix of showcasing your design skills, demonstrating your soft skills, and displaying a strong understanding of the company's products or services. To prepare for interviews, spend time researching the company and familiarizing yourself with their design philosophy and style.

During the interview, be prepared to discuss your design process, walk the interviewer through your portfolio, and explain your rationale behind specific design decisions. Additionally, you may be asked to complete a design exercise or participate in a group activity to gauge your problem-solving and collaboration skills.

Creating a career development plan

As you progress in your UX design career, it's essential to have a plan for your professional growth. Set short-term and long-term goals, identify areas where you'd like to improve, and determine which skills or qualifications may help you advance in your career. Regularly reevaluate and update your career development plan as your goals and priorities change over time.

Understanding the UX design job market is a crucial step in launching your career in this exciting field. By familiarizing yourself with industry growth, types of companies hiring UX designers, roles and responsibilities, and common job titles, you can better position yourself for success. Don't forget the importance of soft skills and staying current with industry trends to ensure you remain competitive in the ever-evolving job market. As you gain experience and refine your skills, continue to develop a career plan that aligns with your professional goals and aspirations.

crafting a tailored resume and cover letter

Navigating the job search process can be challenging, but crafting a tailored resume and cover letter is an essential step in making a great first impression and securing an interview. In this section, we'll discuss strategies for creating a compelling resume and cover letter that showcase your skills and experiences in the best possible light.

Crafting a tailored resume

A well-crafted resume can help you stand out among other applicants and showcase your unique value as a UX designer. Here are some tips for crafting a resume that highlights your skills, experiences, and achievements:

1. Start with a strong summary: Begin your resume with a brief summary that highlights your most relevant skills and experiences. This section should be concise and tailored to the specific job you're applying for. Aim to give the hiring manager a clear sense of your expertise and what you bring to the table.

2. Focus on accomplishments: When describing your work experience, emphasize your accomplishments and the impact you've made in your previous roles. Use concrete numbers and metrics to demonstrate your successes, such as the percentage of increased user engagement or the number of successful product launches you've contributed to.

3. Showcase your design skills: Be sure to include a section dedicated to your design skills, such as wireframing, prototyping, user testing, and interaction design. List the design tools and software you're proficient in, as well as any relevant certifications or courses you've completed.

4. Highlight your soft skills: Soft skills, such as communication, collaboration, and problem-solving, are highly valued in UX design roles. Be sure to mention any experiences that demonstrate your ability to work well with others, manage projects, and adapt to changing circumstances.

5. Keep it concise: Aim for a one- to two-page resume that presents your most relevant and impressive information. Remember that hiring managers may only spend a few seconds skimming each resume, so make sure your content is concise, well-organized, and easy to read.

6. Tailor your resume to the job: Customize your resume for each job application by emphasizing the skills and experiences most relevant to the position. Carefully read the job description and make sure to address any specific requirements mentioned.

Crafting a tailored cover letter

A well-written cover letter can help you stand out from the competition and provide additional context for your resume. Here are some tips for crafting a cover letter that complements your resume and highlights your unique value as a UX designer:

1. Address the hiring manager: Whenever possible, find out the name of the person responsible for hiring and address your cover letter to them directly. This personal touch can help your application feel more genuine and engaging.

2. Open with a strong introduction: Begin your cover letter with a compelling introduction that grabs the reader's attention and encourages them to continue reading. In this section, briefly explain why you're interested in the position and how your skills and experiences make you a great fit.

3. Tell a story: Use your cover letter to tell a story about your career journey and what led you to become a UX designer. Highlight specific experiences or projects that demonstrate your passion for UX design and your ability to make a meaningful impact in the field.

4. Explain your value: Clearly articulate how your skills, experiences, and personal qualities would make you a valuable addition to the company. Be specific about how you can contribute to the organization's goals and help them solve their design challenges.

5. Keep it focused: Like your resume, your cover letter should be concise and focused on the most relevant information. Aim for a one-page letter that is easy to read and engages the reader from start to finish.

6. Close with a call to action: In your closing paragraph, express your enthusiasm for the opportunity and invite the hiring manager to get in touch with you to discuss the position further. Provide your contact information and mention that

you'd be happy to provide additional materials, such as a portfolio or references, upon request.

7. Proofread and edit: Before sending your cover letter, carefully proofread and edit it for grammar, spelling, and punctuation errors. Consider asking a friend or mentor to review your letter and provide feedback on its content and tone.

8. Tailor your cover letter to the job: Just like your resume, it's essential to customize your cover letter for each job application. Refer to the specific job description and use the same language and keywords to show that you've done your research and understand the company's needs.

9. Showcase your passion for the company: Demonstrate that you've researched the company and its products or services. Share what you admire about the organization and explain how your values and goals align with theirs. This can help you stand out as a candidate who is not only passionate about UX design but also committed to the company's mission and vision.

10. Include a strong closing: End your cover letter on a positive and confident note. Reiterate your interest in the position and your belief in your ability to contribute to the company's success. Thank them for considering your application and express your eagerness to discuss the opportunity further.

By crafting a tailored resume and cover letter that highlight your unique skills, experiences, and passion for UX design, you can increase your chances of catching the attention of hiring managers and securing an interview.

ux design interview formats

Getting ready for a UX design interview can be an exciting and nerve-wracking experience. To help you prepare, let's take a look at the various interview formats you may encounter as a UX designer. Understanding these formats can help you feel more confident and ensure you're well-prepared for any situation.

1. Phone or video interviews: In the early stages of the hiring process, companies often conduct phone or video interviews to screen candidates. These interviews typically focus on general topics, such as your background, experience, and interest in the company. Be prepared to discuss your resume, your design process, and your motivation for applying to the position. Make sure you have a quiet, comfortable space with a reliable internet connection for video interviews.

2. In-person interviews: In-person interviews are an opportunity for hiring managers to get to know you better and dive deeper into your skills and experiences. These interviews can be more formal and structured, or they may have a more casual and conversational tone. Expect to answer questions about your portfolio, specific projects you've worked on, and your approach to problem-solving. You might also be asked about your teamwork, communication, and time management skills.

3. Technical interviews: Technical interviews are designed to assess your knowledge of UX design principles, tools, and technologies. In these interviews, you may be asked to solve problems, answer technical questions, or perform tasks that demonstrate your expertise. Be prepared to discuss

topics such as user research, information architecture, interaction design, and usability testing. You might also be asked about your familiarity with specific design tools, such as Sketch, Figma, or Adobe XD.

4. Whiteboard challenges: Whiteboard challenges are a common interview format in the UX design field. In these exercises, you'll be asked to sketch out a design solution to a given problem on a whiteboard or a large sheet of paper. These challenges are meant to assess your problem-solving abilities, creativity, and ability to think on your feet. Practice sketching out ideas quickly and coherently, and be prepared to explain your thought process as you work through the challenge.

5. Take-home design exercises: Some companies might ask you to complete a take-home design exercise as part of the interview process. These assignments usually involve designing a specific feature or solving a problem related to the company's product or service. You'll typically be given a few days to complete the exercise and then present your solution during a follow-up interview. Make sure to follow the given guidelines, pay attention to detail, and showcase your design process in your submission.

6. Portfolio reviews: A portfolio review is an essential part of any UX design interview. During these reviews, you'll be asked to present and discuss your work, including specific projects and case studies. Be prepared to explain the goals, challenges, and solutions for each project, as well as the design process you followed. You should also be ready to discuss your role on the team, the tools you used, and the outcomes of the project.

7. Behavioral interviews: Behavioral interviews are designed to assess how you've handled specific situations in the past. Interviewers will ask you questions about your experiences and how you've managed various challenges, such as working with difficult team members, meeting tight deadlines, or resolving conflicts. To prepare for these questions, think about your past experiences and come up with examples that demonstrate your problem-solving skills, adaptability, and resilience.

8. Group interviews: In some cases, you might be invited to a group interview with other candidates. This format can help employers assess your ability to work in a team, communicate effectively, and handle group dynamics. Be prepared to collaborate with others, share your ideas, and listen to the perspectives of your fellow candidates.

By familiarizing yourself with these interview formats, you can be better prepared to tackle any UX design interview with confidence. Here are a few additional tips to help you excel in each format:

1. Practice active listening: Regardless of the interview format, it's essential to listen carefully to the questions asked and respond thoughtfully. Active listening demonstrates your ability to engage in effective communication and shows your genuine interest in the conversation.

2. Do your research: Before any interview, research the company, its products, services, and target audience. This knowledge will help you tailor your answers to demonstrate how your skills and experience align with the company's needs and goals.

3. Tell stories: When discussing your experiences, try to frame them as stories that highlight your accomplishments, problem-solving abilities, and growth. Stories are more memorable and engaging than simply listing facts, and they can help set you apart from other candidates.

4. Show enthusiasm: Convey your passion for UX design and your excitement about the opportunity to work with the company. Employers want to hire people who are genuinely interested in their work and will bring energy and commitment to the role.

5. Ask insightful questions: Come prepared with thoughtful questions to ask the interviewer. This not only shows that you've done your homework but also gives you valuable insights into the company culture, team dynamics, and expectations for the role.

6. Practice self-reflection: Before your interview, think about your strengths, weaknesses, and areas for improvement. Be prepared to discuss these openly and honestly, as well as how you plan to address any gaps in your skills or experience.

7. Be yourself: Finally, remember to be authentic and true to yourself during the interview. Employers want to get to know the real you, so it's essential to let your personality shine through.

By keeping these tips in mind and being well-prepared for various interview formats, you can confidently navigate the UX design job market and land your dream role.

preparing for common ux design interview questions

As you embark on your journey to becoming a UX designer, one of the most critical aspects of the job-seeking process is the interview. To help you ace your UX design interviews, let's explore some common questions you may encounter and discuss how to prepare thoughtful and impressive answers.

1. What interests you about UX design?

This question helps interviewers understand your motivation and passion for UX design. To answer this question, consider sharing your thoughts on how UX design impacts people's lives, specific aspects of the field that excite you, and any personal experiences that led you to pursue a career in UX design.

1. Can you walk us through your design process?

Interviewers often ask this question to gauge your approach to problem-solving and to assess your ability to articulate your design process. To answer this question, describe the various stages you follow when working on a project, such as research, ideation, prototyping, testing, and iteration. Be sure to mention any specific tools or methods you use and explain why they are helpful.

How do you approach user research?

This question helps interviewers understand your methods for collecting and analyzing user data. Describe the different research techniques you employ, such as interviews, surveys, and usability testing, and explain how you use this information to inform your design decisions. Don't forget to highlight the importance of empathy and understanding users' needs, goals, and pain points.

Sarah Michaels

How do you handle conflicting feedback from stakeholders or users?

Handling feedback is a crucial skill for UX designers, as
it's essential to balance the needs of various stakeholders
while maintaining a user-centric focus. In your response,
emphasize the importance of open communication, active
listening, and collaboration. Explain how you prioritize feedback, seek clarification when necessary, and iterate on your
designs to find the best solution for all parties involved.

- Can you describe a challenging project you've
  worked on and how you overcame those
  challenges?

This question allows interviewers to learn about your
problem-solving skills, adaptability, and resilience. Choose a
project where you faced significant obstacles, such as tight
deadlines, conflicting requirements, or limited resources.
Discuss the specific challenges you encountered, how you
addressed them, and what you learned from the experience.

- How do you stay current with industry trends and
  best practices in UX design?

As a UX designer, it's vital to keep up with the ever-
evolving field. Share the resources you use to stay informed,
such as blogs, podcasts, conferences, and online courses. Also,
mention any professional organizations or networking groups
you participate in to connect with other UX professionals and
learn from their experiences.

- How do you ensure accessibility in your designs?

Accessibility is a critical consideration in UX design, as it
ensures that your products are usable by a diverse range of

people, including those with disabilities. Explain your approach to incorporating accessibility principles into your designs, such as using appropriate color contrasts, providing alternative text for images, and following established guidelines like the Web Content Accessibility Guidelines (WCAG).

- How do you collaborate with other team members, such as developers, product managers, and graphic designers?

UX design often involves working closely with a multidisciplinary team. Highlight your communication and teamwork skills by explaining how you establish clear expectations, share your design rationale, and seek input from others throughout the design process. Emphasize your ability to adapt to different working styles and your willingness to learn from your colleagues.

As you prepare for your UX design interviews, remember that practice makes perfect. Take the time to reflect on your experiences, think about the lessons you've learned, and consider how you can best articulate your unique perspective and approach to UX design.

In conclusion, don't forget that interviews are a two-way street. Use this opportunity to ask thoughtful questions about the company, team, and role to ensure it s a good fit for you as well. By showing genuine curiosity and interest in the organization, you'll not only gain valuable insights but also demonstrate your enthusiasm for the position.

Now that you're armed with an understanding of common UX design interview questions, let's explore a few additional tips to help you make a positive impression:

1. Showcase your adaptability and growth mindset:
   UX design is a constantly evolving field, and interviewers will be looking for candidates who can

adapt and grow with it. Be prepared to discuss how you've learned from past experiences and how you continually strive to improve your skills and knowledge.

2. Provide concrete examples: When answering interview questions, use specific examples from your past experiences to illustrate your points. This helps paint a clear picture of your skills and abilities, making it easier for interviewers to envision how you'd contribute to their team.

3. Highlight your soft skills: While technical proficiency is essential in UX design, soft skills like communication, collaboration, and problem-solving are equally important. Be sure to emphasize these skills throughout your interview and provide examples of how they've contributed to your success.

4. Practice your storytelling: Interviewers often remember stories more than facts or figures. As you prepare for your interview, think about how you can weave engaging narratives around your experiences, projects, and accomplishments. This will make your responses more memorable and help you stand out from other candidates.

5. Prepare a list of thoughtful questions: As mentioned earlier, interviews are an opportunity for you to learn about the company and role. Come prepared with a list of questions that demonstrate your research and interest in the organization. This will not only help you make an informed decision about the job offer but also leave a positive impression on the interviewers.

6. Don't forget to follow up: After your interview, send a thank-you email to express your gratitude for the opportunity and reiterate your interest in

the position. This small gesture can go a long way in leaving a positive impression and keeping you top-of-mind with the hiring team.

By diligently preparing for common UX design interview questions and following these additional tips, you'll be well on your way to landing your dream job in UX design.

tips for successful interviews

Stepping into the world of UX design can be incredibly rewarding, but it's also a competitive field. To land that dream job, it's essential to excel not only in your technical skills but also in your interview performance. With that in mind, let's dive into some tips and strategies for ensuring successful interviews in the UX design field.

1. Do your homework: Before you even step foot in the interview room, take the time to research the company and the role you're applying for thoroughly. Familiarize yourself with the organization's mission, values, and culture, as well as the specific projects they're working on. This will allow you to tailor your responses to align with the company's goals and demonstrate your genuine interest in the position.

2. Practice active listening: While it's natural to focus on what you're going to say next during an interview, don't forget to actively listen to your interviewer. By paying close attention to their questions and comments, you'll be able to provide thoughtful, relevant responses that address their specific concerns.

3. Dress appropriately: First impressions matter, and dressing professionally for your interview will

show that you're serious about the position. Opt for business casual attire that is neat, clean, and well-fitted. Remember, it's always better to be slightly overdressed than underdressed.

4. Be punctual: Arriving late for an interview can be a deal-breaker. Plan your route in advance and aim to arrive at least 15 minutes early, giving yourself time to account for any unforeseen delays. This will also give you a chance to collect your thoughts and calm any pre-interview nerves.

5. Showcase your process: As a UX designer, your thought process and approach to problem-solving are just as important as the final product. During your interview, be prepared to discuss your design process in detail, including how you gather user feedback, iterate on designs, and collaborate with other team members.

6. Bring a polished portfolio: Your portfolio is a visual representation of your skills and experiences, so make sure it's up-to-date and well-organized. Be prepared to walk your interviewer through your portfolio, discussing the goals, challenges, and outcomes of each project. Focus on the projects that best showcase your skills and align with the company's objectives.

7. Demonstrate your passion for UX design: Enthusiasm can be contagious, and showing genuine passion for your work can help you stand out among other candidates. Share your motivations for pursuing a career in UX design, as well as any personal projects or industry events that you've been involved in.

8. Emphasize collaboration and teamwork: UX design is a highly collaborative field, and interviewers will be looking for candidates who can work well with

others. Be sure to highlight your experience working in teams and discuss specific examples of how you've collaborated effectively to achieve project goals.

9. Prepare for behavioral questions: In addition to technical questions, you'll likely encounter behavioral questions designed to assess your soft skills and how you'd fit into the company culture. Practice your responses to common behavioral questions, using the STAR (Situation, Task, Action, Result) method to structure your answers.

10. Stay calm and composed: Even if you're feeling nervous, try to project an air of confidence and professionalism during your interview. Take deep breaths, maintain good eye contact, and speak clearly and calmly. Remember, the interview is an opportunity for both you and the employer to determine if the role is a good fit, so try to approach it as a conversation rather than an interrogation.

As you wrap up your interview, don't forget to express your gratitude for the opportunity and reiterate your interest in the position. Be sure to follow up with a thank-you email, which can serve as a gentle reminder of your application and showcase your professionalism.

1. Ask insightful questions: The interview is not just about the employer evaluating you – it's also your chance to determine if the company and the role are the right fit for you. Prepare a list of thoughtful questions to ask during the interview. These questions should reflect your research on the company and the position, as well as demonstrate your curiosity about the team, company culture, and projects you'd be working on.

2. Show adaptability: UX design is a constantly evolving field, so it's important to demonstrate your willingness to learn and adapt to new techniques, tools, and methodologies. Share examples of how you've adapted to change in previous roles or projects, and express your eagerness to continue learning and growing as a UX designer.

3. Be yourself: While it's important to be professional during an interview, don't be afraid to let your personality shine through. Employers want to hire someone who will be a good cultural fit for their team, so being genuine and authentic can help you stand out from the competition.

4. Address any gaps or weaknesses: If there are gaps in your resume or areas where you lack experience, be prepared to address them during the interview. Instead of trying to hide or downplay these issues, demonstrate self-awareness and a proactive approach to addressing them, such as taking courses or engaging in side projects to gain the necessary skills.

5. Reflect on your experiences: After each interview, take the time to reflect on your performance and identify areas where you could improve. This self-assessment will help you refine your interview technique and increase your chances of success in future interviews.

In the competitive field of UX design, it's crucial to approach interviews with confidence and professionalism. By following these tips and strategies, you'll be well on your way to landing your dream UX design role.

6 /
navigating your ux design career

types of ux design roles

WELCOME to another exciting section of our journey through the world of UX design! In this section, we'll explore the diverse landscape of UX design roles, which can vary widely in terms of responsibilities, skills, and areas of expertise. By understanding the nuances of these roles, you'll be better equipped to pinpoint your strengths and interests, and ultimately find the perfect fit for your career.

1. UX Designer: The most common and general role in the UX design field is the UX Designer. This position entails understanding user needs, designing user interfaces, creating wireframes and prototypes, and collaborating with other team members to create seamless user experiences. UX Designers should have strong problem-solving skills, a deep understanding of user-centered design principles, and proficiency in various design tools and software.

2. UX Researcher: UX Researchers focus on understanding user behavior, preferences, and

motivations through various research methods. These professionals analyze data, conduct user interviews, perform usability testing, and create user personas to help inform the design process. To excel in this role, a UX Researcher should possess strong analytical skills, excellent communication abilities, and a passion for understanding human behavior.

3. Information Architect (IA): Information Architects are responsible for organizing and structuring the content and information within digital products, ensuring that users can easily navigate and find what they're looking for. IAs work closely with UX Designers and Content Strategists, creating sitemaps, taxonomies, and wireframes to help guide the design process. Strong organizational skills, attention to detail, and knowledge of user-centered design principles are crucial for this role.

4. Interaction Designer: Interaction Designers specialize in crafting the behavior and interactions between users and digital products. They focus on creating intuitive, engaging, and efficient interfaces by designing the flow, animations, and micro-interactions that occur within a product. To be successful in this role, an Interaction Designer should have a strong understanding of UX design principles, excellent visual design skills, and proficiency in tools for prototyping and animation.

5. Visual/UI Designer: Visual/UI Designers are responsible for the aesthetic aspects of a digital product, ensuring that the interface is visually appealing, consistent, and aligns with the overall brand identity. These designers work closely with UX Designers and Interaction Designers, focusing on typography, color schemes, icons, and other

visual elements. A keen eye for detail, strong visual design skills, and proficiency in design software are essential for this role.

6. UX Writer: UX Writers create the copy and content that users encounter within digital products. They focus on crafting clear, concise, and engaging language that guides users through their interactions and supports the overall user experience. UX Writers collaborate with UX Designers, Content Strategists, and other team members to ensure that the content aligns with the product's goals and objectives. Excellent writing, editing, and communication skills are crucial for this role.

7. Content Strategist: Content Strategists are responsible for planning, creating, and managing the content within digital products. They work with UX Designers, Information Architects, and other team members to ensure that content meets user needs, supports business objectives, and maintains consistency across the product. Strong organizational and communication skills, a deep understanding of content creation, and the ability to work collaboratively are important qualities for a Content Strategist.

8. UX Strategist: UX Strategists focus on the big picture, helping to define the overall direction and goals of a digital product or service. They work closely with stakeholders, business analysts, and UX teams to ensure that the user experience aligns with business objectives and user needs. A background in business strategy, excellent communication skills, and the ability to balance user and business requirements are essential for success in this role.

9. UX/UI Developer: UX/UI Developers bridge the gap between design and development, transforming design concepts into functional and interactive digital products. They collaborate with UX Designers, UI Designers, and developers, using coding languages such as HTML, CSS, and JavaScript to bring designs to life. Proficiency in front-end development, an understanding of UX design principles, and strong problem-solving skills are vital for this role.

10. UX Manager/Team Lead: UX Managers and Team Leads oversee and coordinate the work of UX teams, ensuring that projects are completed on time and meet quality standards. They are responsible for providing guidance, mentorship, and direction to their team members, as well as communicating with stakeholders and other departments within the organization. Strong leadership, project management, and communication skills are crucial for success in this role.

11. UX Consultant: UX Consultants work independently or as part of a consulting firm, providing expert advice and guidance to clients on UX design projects. They may be brought in to assess existing products, provide recommendations for improvement, or help with the planning and execution of new projects. A solid background in UX design, strong communication skills, and the ability to adapt to different clients and industries are important qualities for a UX Consultant.

As you can see, there are a wide variety of roles within the UX design field, each with its own unique set of responsibilities and skills. As you embark on your journey to becoming a UX professional, take the time to explore these different roles and consider which best aligns with your strengths, interests, and career goals.

finding the right company culture and work environment

Diving into the world of UX design, you'll soon discover that no two companies or work environments are exactly the same. Just as you've spent time carefully considering which UX design role best suits your skills and interests, you'll also need to put thought into finding the right company culture and work environment that aligns with your values and aspirations. In this section, we'll explore some key factors to consider as you search for the perfect fit.

1. Company Size: Companies come in all shapes and sizes, from small startups to large, established corporations. Each size offers unique advantages and challenges. Smaller companies may provide more opportunities for hands-on experience, a greater sense of camaraderie, and the chance to have a significant impact on the organization's direction. On the other hand, larger companies can offer more resources, a wider range of projects and clients, and opportunities for upward mobility. Reflect on your preferences and consider which size may be the best match for your personality and career goals.

2. Industry: UX designers can find opportunities in a wide range of industries, from tech and healthcare to finance and entertainment. As you research potential employers, think about which industries excite you the most and where you believe you can make the greatest impact. Consider how the industry might affect the types of projects you'll

work on, as well as the overall pace and work environment.

3. Mission and Values: It's important to find a company whose mission and values resonate with you. Look for organizations that share your passion for user-centric design and have a strong commitment to creating exceptional experiences for their users. Pay attention to the company's stated values and how they align with your own, as this can greatly impact your job satisfaction and overall happiness in the workplace.

4. Work-Life Balance: The work environment and expectations can vary significantly from company to company. Some organizations may emphasize long hours and a fast-paced, high-pressure atmosphere, while others prioritize a healthy work-life balance and flexible schedules. Reflect on your preferences and determine the type of work environment that will best support your well-being and allow you to thrive.

5. Opportunities for Growth and Development: As a UX professional, it's important to stay on top of industry trends and continuously expand your skillset. Seek out companies that value professional development and provide opportunities for training, mentorship, and career advancement. This will not only help you stay relevant in the field but also foster a sense of personal fulfillment and accomplishment.

6. Collaboration and Team Dynamics: UX design is a highly collaborative field, requiring designers to work closely with colleagues across various departments. As you research potential employers, take note of their approach to collaboration and team dynamics. Do they foster a supportive,

inclusive environment that encourages open communication and the sharing of ideas? Or is the atmosphere more competitive and individualistic? Consider which approach best aligns with your own working style and preferences.

7. Remote or In-Office Work: The rise of remote work has provided more flexibility for many professionals, including UX designers. Some companies may offer fully remote positions, while others may require you to work in an office or offer a hybrid model. Reflect on your preferred work setup and how it might impact your productivity, job satisfaction, and overall well-being.

8. Benefits and Compensation: While salary is certainly an important factor to consider, don't forget to evaluate the overall benefits package offered by potential employers. This may include health insurance, retirement plans, paid time off, and other perks such as wellness programs or professional development opportunities. Weigh the value of these benefits against your personal needs and priorities to help determine the best fit for you.

9. Networking and Community Involvement: A company that encourages and supports its employees to participate in industry events, conferences, and meetups can provide valuable opportunities for networking and professional growth. Look for employers that not only sponsor such events but also encourage employees to contribute their expertise by speaking, mentoring, or volunteering. This not only elevates your professional profile but also demonstrates the company's commitment to the UX community.

10. Company Reputation: When evaluating potential employers, it's essential to consider their reputation

within the industry and among their clients. Research the company's track record for producing high-quality work, their commitment to innovation, and their overall impact on the UX design field. You can glean this information from client testimonials, industry awards, or by speaking with current and former employees.

11. Employee Retention and Satisfaction: A high employee retention rate can be an indicator of a positive work environment and company culture. Look for companies with low turnover rates, as this may suggest that employees are happy, well-supported, and enjoy working there. You can often find information about employee satisfaction through company review websites or by connecting with current and former employees on professional networking platforms.

12. Mentorship Opportunities: As a UX designer, having access to experienced mentors can be invaluable for your professional growth. Seek out companies that have strong mentorship programs or emphasize collaboration between junior and senior team members. These opportunities will not only help you improve your skills but also build strong professional relationships that can benefit your career in the long run.

Finding the right company culture and work environment involves a careful evaluation of various factors such as company size, industry, mission and values, work-life balance, opportunities for growth, team dynamics, and more. By taking the time to research and reflect on your preferences, you'll be better equipped to identify the ideal workplace that will support your professional and personal growth as a UX designer.

advancing your career through professional development

In this section, we will discuss the importance of professional development and how it can help you advance your career as a UX designer. We'll explore various avenues for learning and growth, from attending workshops and conferences to obtaining certifications and honing your skills through personal projects. Let's dive in!

1. Continuing Education: As a UX designer, it's crucial to stay current with industry trends, best practices, and new technologies. One way to ensure you're keeping up-to-date is by pursuing continuing education opportunities. These can include workshops, seminars, online courses, and even degree programs. By dedicating time to learning, you'll not only sharpen your existing skills but also acquire new ones that will make you more valuable in the job market.

2. Networking: Networking is an essential aspect of professional development. Attending industry events, conferences, and local meetups allows you to connect with other professionals, exchange ideas, and learn from their experiences. Building a strong professional network can lead to new job opportunities, collaborations, and access to valuable resources and information.

3. Certifications: Obtaining industry-recognized certifications can help you stand out from the competition and demonstrate your commitment to professional growth. There are several UX design certifications available, such as the Interaction Design Foundation (IDF) courses, the Certified User Experience Analyst (CXA) from the UX

Certification Board, and the Nielsen Norman Group (NNG) UX Certification. Earning these credentials can boost your credibility and open doors to new job opportunities.

4. Joining Professional Organizations: Becoming a member of professional organizations, such as the User Experience Professionals Association (UXPA) or the Interaction Design Association (IxDA), can provide numerous benefits for your career development. These organizations offer access to exclusive resources, networking events, and learning opportunities. They also provide opportunities to collaborate on projects, engage in mentorship programs, and participate in local sections.

5. Speaking and Presenting: Sharing your expertise by speaking at conferences, webinars, or local meetups can help establish you as a thought leader in the UX design community. This not only raises your professional profile but also provides an opportunity to give back to the community, contribute to the industry's collective knowledge, and refine your communication skills.

6. Writing and Publishing: Another way to advance your career is by writing and publishing articles, blog posts, or even books on UX design topics. Sharing your insights and experiences not only helps others learn but also solidifies your understanding of the subject matter. Additionally, having a portfolio of published work showcases your expertise and can attract the attention of potential employers.

7. Mentorship: Serving as a mentor or seeking mentorship can be highly beneficial to your professional growth. As a mentor, you can guide

and inspire others while reflecting on your own experiences and gaining a fresh perspective on your work. As a mentee, you can learn from seasoned professionals, gain insights into their thought processes, and benefit from their guidance and expertise.

8. Personal Projects: Working on personal projects is an excellent way to develop and refine your UX design skills. These projects can range from redesigning an existing product or website to creating a new app or service from scratch. Not only do personal projects provide an opportunity to practice and experiment with new techniques, but they can also be included in your portfolio to showcase your abilities.

9. Staying Informed: Regularly reading industry news, following UX design blogs, and engaging in online forums can help you stay informed about the latest trends, tools, and best practices. By staying up-to-date, you'll be better prepared to adapt to changes in the industry and continue to grow as a professional.

10. Soft Skills Development: While technical skills are essential for a UX designer, developing soft skills such as communication, collaboration, and empathy can significantly contribute to your career advancement. Consider taking workshops or courses that focus on improving these skills, as they will not only make you a more effective designer but also a better team player and leader.

11. Embracing Feedback: Actively seeking feedback from peers, mentors, and even clients can help you identify areas for improvement and growth. Be open to constructive criticism and use it as an opportunity to learn and enhance your UX design

skills. By embracing feedback, you demonstrate your commitment to continuous improvement and professional development.

12. Teaching and Training: Sharing your knowledge with others by teaching workshops, leading training sessions, or even creating online courses can help you solidify your understanding of UX design concepts while also positioning you as an expert in your field. Teaching others not only contributes to the growth of the UX community but also helps you refine your own skills and understanding.

13. Time Management: Effective time management is crucial for any professional, including UX designers. Learning how to prioritize tasks, set realistic goals, and manage your workload can significantly impact your productivity and your ability to grow in your career. Consider implementing productivity techniques such as the Pomodoro Technique or time blocking to help you stay focused and organized.

14. Setting Goals and Tracking Progress: Establishing clear career goals and tracking your progress is essential for professional development. Take the time to reflect on your accomplishments, identify areas for improvement, and set both short-term and long-term goals for yourself. Regularly reviewing and updating your goals will help you stay motivated and ensure that you're on the right path for career advancement.

15. Work-Life Balance: Lastly, remember that maintaining a healthy work-life balance is crucial for sustainable career growth. While it's essential to be committed to your professional development, it's equally important to prioritize self-care and

personal well-being. Taking breaks, engaging in hobbies, and spending time with loved ones can help prevent burnout and keep you energized for continued growth in your UX design career.

By incorporating these strategies into your professional journey, you'll be well on your way to advancing your career in UX design.

expanding your skillset and staying current

Welcome back, my friend! In this section, we'll dive into the importance of expanding your skillset and staying current in the ever-evolving world of UX design. As a UX designer, it's crucial to continually learn and grow to ensure you're providing the best possible user experiences and staying competitive in the job market. So, let's explore various ways to expand your skills, stay up-to-date with industry trends, and remain a valuable asset in the UX design community.

1. Keep Learning: First and foremost, never stop learning. UX design is an ever-evolving field, and to stay relevant, you must be willing to invest in your ongoing education. Attend workshops, webinars, and conferences to learn about the latest tools, techniques, and best practices in the field. Read books, articles, and research papers to deepen your understanding of UX design principles and methodologies.

2. Online Courses and Tutorials: One of the easiest ways to expand your skillset is by taking online courses and following tutorials. Many platforms offer courses on various UX design topics, allowing you to learn at your own pace and from the comfort of your home. Choose courses that complement

your existing knowledge or focus on specific areas you'd like to improve or explore.

3. Diversify Your Skills: While it's essential to specialize in certain areas of UX design, having a diverse skillset can make you a more versatile and valuable designer. Consider learning complementary skills such as UI design, graphic design, front-end development, or even copywriting. These additional skills will enable you to work on a broader range of projects and collaborate more effectively with multidisciplinary teams.

4. Stay Informed About Industry Trends: To stay current in the UX design field, it's crucial to keep an eye on industry trends and emerging technologies. Subscribe to industry newsletters, follow influential UX designers and organizations on social media, and join UX design forums and communities. By staying informed, you'll be better equipped to adapt to changes in the industry and incorporate new ideas into your work.

5. Participate in Design Challenges: Design challenges and hackathons are fantastic opportunities to learn new skills, work on real-world problems, and collaborate with other designers. By participating in these events, you'll be able to put your skills to the test, learn from others, and expand your professional network.

6. Collaborate with Other Designers: Working with other designers can help you learn new techniques, gain fresh perspectives, and sharpen your problem-solving abilities. Engage in collaborative projects, participate in design critiques, or even form a UX design study group. Learning from your peers is an invaluable way to grow and expand your skillset.

7. Practice, Practice, Practice: As with any skill, practice is essential for growth and improvement in UX design. Work on personal projects, freelance assignments, or contribute to open-source initiatives to hone your skills and build your portfolio. The more you practice, the more confident and proficient you'll become as a UX designer.

8. Obtain Certifications: Earning UX design certifications can help you validate your skills, demonstrate your expertise, and stand out in the job market. Pursue certifications from reputable organizations such as the Interaction Design Foundation, Nielsen Norman Group, or Human Factors International. By earning these certifications, you'll not only enhance your resume but also deepen your understanding of UX design principles and best practices.

9. Learn from Industry Leaders: Identify UX design leaders and influencers who inspire you, and follow their work. Attend their talks, read their books and articles, and engage with them on social media. Learning from the experiences and insights of industry leaders can provide invaluable guidance for your own professional journey.

10. Reflect and Evaluate: Periodically take a step back and assess your progress, skillset, and goals. Reflect on your strengths and weaknesses, and identify areas where you need to improve or expand your skills. This self-evaluation will help you set realistic goals and guide your ongoing professional development efforts.

11. Teach and Mentor Others: Sharing your knowledge and experience with others can help you solidify your understanding and develop your

communication skills. Offer to mentor junior designers, lead workshops, or contribute articles and tutorials to design publications. Teaching others not only benefits the UX design community, but it also helps you grow and refine your skills.

12. Embrace Change and Adaptability: The UX design landscape is constantly changing, and it's essential to be adaptable and open to change. Be willing to learn new tools, embrace new methodologies, and adjust your design approach as needed. This adaptability will not only make you a more resilient designer, but it will also ensure you stay current with the ever-evolving field of UX design.

13. Develop a Growth Mindset: Finally, cultivate a growth mindset that embraces learning, curiosity, and continuous improvement. Recognize that mistakes and setbacks are opportunities to learn and grow. By adopting this mindset, you'll be more open to exploring new ideas, taking risks, and embracing challenges.

Now that we've discussed various strategies for expanding your skillset and staying current in the UX design field, it's up to you to take the initiative and invest in your ongoing professional development. Remember, the most successful UX designers are lifelong learners who continually seek to improve their skills, adapt to changes in the industry, and stay ahead of the curve.

As you embark on your journey of growth and continuous learning, keep in mind that this is a marathon, not a sprint. Focus on steady, consistent progress, and celebrate your achievements along the way. By committing to your professional development and staying current in the field of UX design, you'll be well-equipped to navigate the ever-changing landscape and forge a successful, fulfilling career.

And there you have it! We've covered a wide range of strategies to help you expand your skillset and stay current in the exciting and ever-evolving world of UX design. Keep these tips in mind as you continue to develop your career, and remember: the most important thing is to stay curious, keep learning, and never stop growing. Good luck, and happy designing!

conclusion

embracing the ux designer mindset

Welcome back! In this section, we're going to discuss the importance of building a professional network and share some strategies to help you connect with other UX design professionals, expand your circle of influence, and ultimately advance your career.

Why is building a professional network important?

A strong professional network can be an invaluable resource throughout your UX design career. Here are a few reasons why building a network should be a priority:

1. Access to Job Opportunities: Many job openings are never advertised publicly, instead being filled through word of mouth or personal connections. Having an extensive professional network increases your chances of hearing about these "hidden" opportunities.
2. Learning and Growth: Connecting with other professionals can help you learn about new techniques, tools, and trends in the UX design field.

By sharing knowledge and experiences, you can gain new insights and improve your skills.

3. Collaboration and Support: A supportive network can provide encouragement, advice, and feedback as you navigate your career. Collaborating with others can lead to new projects, partnerships, and professional growth.

4. Increased Visibility: Networking can help you become more visible within the UX design community, which can lead to more job offers, speaking engagements, and other opportunities.

Now that we've discussed the importance of building a professional network, let's explore some strategies to help you create and maintain meaningful connections with other UX design professionals.

1. Attend Conferences and Industry Events: UX design conferences and events are excellent opportunities to meet other professionals, learn about the latest trends, and expand your network. Make an effort to attend local, national, or even international conferences and events whenever possible. Be sure to introduce yourself to others, exchange contact information, and follow up after the event.

2. Join UX Design Groups and Communities: There are many online and offline communities dedicated to UX design. Seek out local meetups, online forums, and social media groups where you can connect with others who share your passion for UX design. Participate in discussions, ask questions, and share your knowledge to build relationships within these communities.

3. Leverage Social Media: Use social media platforms like LinkedIn, Twitter, and Facebook to connect with other UX design professionals. Share your work, engage in discussions, and follow influencers in the field to stay up to date on industry news and trends.

4. Connect with Alumni: Reach out to fellow graduates from your UX design program or bootcamp. They may be able to introduce you to other professionals in the field, share job opportunities, or provide insights into the UX design job market.

5. Collaborate on Projects: Seek out opportunities to work with other UX designers on projects, either professionally or as a side project. Collaborating on projects allows you to build relationships while also learning from others and improving your skills.

6. Offer Help and Support: Be willing to help others when they need assistance, whether it's by providing feedback on their work, sharing job leads, or offering a listening ear. By being a supportive and helpful member of the community, you'll build goodwill and strengthen your relationships.

7. Keep in Touch: Building a professional network isn't a one-time effort; it requires ongoing maintenance. Stay in touch with your contacts, share updates about your career, and check in with them periodically. This will help you maintain strong connections and ensure your network continues to grow.

8. Network Authentically: Remember that networking is about building genuine relationships, not just collecting business cards or LinkedIn connections. Focus on getting to know others, understanding

their needs, and finding ways to support them. By being authentic and genuine in your networking efforts, you'll create stronger, more meaningful connections.

As we wrap up this section, remember that building a professional network is an ongoing process that requires time, effort, and patience. However, the benefits of having a strong professional network in the UX design community are well worth the investment. As you grow your network and deepen your connections, you'll find that your career opportunities, learning experiences, and professional support system will expand, helping you achieve greater success in your UX design journey.

In summary, building a professional network is crucial for your career development in UX design. It can provide you with access to job opportunities, valuable learning experiences, collaboration, and increased visibility in the industry. To build and maintain a strong network, make sure to:

1. Attend conferences and industry events.
2. Join UX design groups and communities.
3. Leverage social media to connect with professionals.
4. Connect with alumni from your UX design program or bootcamp.
5. Collaborate on projects with other designers.
6. Offer help and support to others in your network.
7. Keep in touch with your contacts.
8. Network authentically and genuinely.

Remember, networking is a continuous process, and the more you engage with others in the UX design community, the more valuable your network will become. Keep refining your networking skills, and stay proactive in seeking out new connections and opportunities.

As you move forward in your UX design career, always make it a priority to invest in your professional network. The relationships you build, the knowledge you gain, and the experiences you share with others in the field will help shape your career trajectory and ultimately contribute to your long-term success in the world of UX design.

the journey of lifelong learning and growth

As you embark on your UX design career, it's important to remember that learning and growth don't stop once you land your first job or reach a certain level of expertise. In fact, the most successful UX designers are those who approach their careers as a journey of lifelong learning and growth. This section will explore the importance of continuous learning and development, offer strategies for staying current with industry trends and innovations, and provide tips for fostering a growth mindset that will set you up for long-term success in your UX design career.

- The importance of continuous learning and development

In the fast-paced and ever-evolving world of UX design, staying up-to-date with the latest trends, tools, and best practices is crucial for remaining competitive and delivering exceptional user experiences. By committing to continuous learning and development, you'll be better equipped to adapt to the changing landscape of UX design, stay ahead of the curve, and ensure your skills remain relevant and in demand.

Moreover, continuous learning can help you uncover new interests, build expertise in specialized areas, and open up new career opportunities. As you progress in your UX design career, you may find that your interests shift or that new areas of specialization emerge. Embracing lifelong learning allows you to explore these interests and stay engaged with your work, ultimately leading to greater career satisfaction and success.

- Staying current with industry trends and innovations

To stay current with industry trends and innovations, it's important to be proactive in seeking out information and resources. Here are a few strategies for staying up-to-date with the latest developments in the world of UX design:

- Follow industry publications: Subscribe to UX design blogs, magazines, and newsletters to receive regular updates on news, trends, and best practices. Some popular publications include UX Design Weekly, Smashing Magazine, and UX Matters.
- Attend conferences and workshops: Conferences and workshops offer opportunities to learn from industry experts, network with other professionals, and gain exposure to new ideas and techniques. Make it a point to attend at least one or two UX design conferences or workshops each year.
- Participate in online forums and communities: Online forums and communities, such as UX Stack Exchange or UX Design Slack communities, can be invaluable sources of information and support. Participate in discussions, ask questions, and share your own insights to stay engaged with the UX design community.
- Take online courses and attend webinars: Online courses and webinars offer convenient and affordable opportunities to expand your knowledge

and skills. Look for courses and webinars on platforms like Coursera, Udemy, and Skillshare, or through UX design organizations such as the Interaction Design Foundation or the Nielsen Norman Group.

- Setting goals for personal and professional growth

Setting specific, measurable, achievable, relevant, and time-bound (SMART) goals can help you stay focused on your personal and professional growth. Regularly reassess your goals and track your progress, adjusting your objectives as needed to ensure they remain relevant and attainable. Here are a few examples of SMART goals for UX designers:

- "I will complete a UX design course on user research techniques within the next three months."
- "I will attend at least two UX design conferences this year to network and learn about new trends in the industry."
- "I will improve my visual design skills by taking an online course on typography and color theory over the next six weeks."

- Fostering a growth mindset

Developing a growth mindset is crucial for embracing life-long learning and achieving long-term success in your UX design career. A growth mindset is the belief that intelligence and abilities can be developed through dedication and hard work, and that challenges are opportunities for growth. Here are some tips for fostering a growth mindset:

- Embrace challenges: View challenges as opportunities to learn and grow rather than as obstacles to be avoided. When faced with a difficult project or a new tool, approach the situation with curiosity and a willingness to learn.

- Learn from feedback: Constructive criticism is essential for professional growth. Welcome feedback from colleagues, managers, and users, and use it as a tool to improve your work and your skills.
- Celebrate the success of others: Recognize and celebrate the achievements of your peers, and use their accomplishments as inspiration for your own growth. Adopting a collaborative and supportive mindset can help you build strong relationships and foster a positive work environment.
- Be resilient: Understand that setbacks are a natural part of the learning process. When you encounter obstacles or failures, focus on what you can learn from the experience and use that knowledge to inform your future efforts.
- Cultivate curiosity: Stay curious about the UX design field and be open to exploring new ideas, techniques, and tools. By maintaining a curious mindset, you'll be more likely to stay engaged with your work and stay on top of industry trends.

- The rewards of lifelong learning and growth

Embracing lifelong learning and growth in your UX design career offers numerous benefits, both professionally and personally. By continually expanding your knowledge and skills, you'll increase your marketability, open up new career opportunities, and stay relevant in the rapidly evolving world of UX design.

Additionally, engaging in continuous learning can lead to increased job satisfaction, as you'll be better equipped to tackle new challenges and contribute to your team's success. It can also foster a sense of personal accomplishment and boost your self-confidence, as you witness your own growth and development over time.

Ultimately, the journey of lifelong learning and growth is an integral part of a fulfilling and successful career in UX design. By adopting a growth mindset and making a commitment to continuous learning and development, you'll be well on your way to reaching your full potential as a UX designer and making a lasting impact in the field.

As you continue on your UX design journey, remember that learning is an ongoing process. It is your curiosity, dedication, and persistence that will truly set you apart in this exciting and dynamic industry. So, keep pushing forward, embrace new challenges, and always be open to learning from your experiences. The world of UX design is ever-evolving, and your ability to adapt and grow with it will serve you well throughout your career.

making an impact through ux design

Embarking on a career in UX design is more than just a job; it's an opportunity to make a real impact on people's lives through thoughtful and well-crafted experiences. In this section, we'll explore the ways in which UX design can positively influence the world around us and discuss how you, as a UX designer, can contribute to meaningful change through your work.

Enhancing user experiences

One of the most immediate and visible ways UX design makes an impact is by enhancing user experiences. A well-designed product or service can improve people's lives by making everyday tasks more efficient, accessible, and enjoyable. As a UX designer, you have the power to create experiences that delight users and help them accomplish their goals with ease.

Examples of improved user experiences include:

- Simplifying complex processes: Streamlining tasks like online banking or booking a trip can save users time and reduce frustration.
- Enhancing accessibility: Designing products and services that are accessible to a diverse range of users, including those with disabilities, ensures that everyone can benefit from your work.
- Creating enjoyable experiences: Adding elements of fun or delight to everyday tasks can make users feel more engaged and connected to your product.

Encouraging positive behavior change

UX design can also have a more profound and long-lasting impact by influencing users' behavior and encouraging positive change. By understanding users' needs, motivations, and barriers to change, UX designers can create products and services that facilitate healthier, more sustainable, or more socially conscious behaviors.

Examples of UX design-driven behavior change include:

- Promoting healthy habits: Designing tools and interfaces that encourage users to make healthier choices, such as fitness apps that make exercise more enjoyable or meal planning platforms that promote balanced eating.
- Supporting environmental sustainability: Creating products and services that encourage eco-friendly habits, such as apps that help users track and reduce their carbon footprint or platforms that facilitate carpooling and ride-sharing.

- Encouraging social responsibility: Designing experiences that promote empathy, awareness, and action on social issues, such as platforms that connect volunteers with local community projects or apps that educate users about global challenges and ways to help.

Driving business and societal innovation

As a UX designer, you can contribute to business and societal innovation by identifying new opportunities and creating solutions that address unmet needs. Through human-centered design processes, you can uncover insights that inspire novel products, services, or systems that have the potential to disrupt industries and create positive change on a larger scale.

Examples of UX design-driven innovation include:

- Identifying new markets: UX research can uncover untapped user needs or desires, leading to the development of innovative products and services that fill gaps in the market.
- Creating more efficient systems: By examining user journeys and identifying pain points, UX designers can develop solutions that streamline processes, reduce waste, and improve overall efficiency.
- Advancing technology: UX designers play a crucial role in shaping the development of emerging technologies, ensuring that new innovations are user-friendly, accessible, and impactful.

Building empathy and bridging divides

In an increasingly connected world, UX design has the power to bring people together by fostering empathy and understanding. By creating experiences that resonate with diverse user groups, UX designers can help break down barriers, facilitate communication, and promote more inclusive and harmonious societies.

Examples of UX design fostering empathy and connection include:

- Designing for cultural diversity: Creating products and services that cater to users from different cultural backgrounds can help build bridges and promote understanding among diverse groups.
- Facilitating communication: Designing tools and platforms that enable more effective communication between users, such as translation apps or platforms for global collaboration, can help foster empathy and understanding.
- Encouraging perspective-taking: Designing experiences that immerse users in different perspectives, such as virtual reality experiences that simulate the lives of others, can promote empathy and challenge biases.

Championing ethical design and responsible technology

As a UX designer, you have the responsibility to advocate for ethical design and responsible technology. By considering the potential consequences of your design decisions and prioritizing user well-being, privacy, and security, you can help create a more ethical and sustainable tech landscape.

Examples of ethical design and responsible technology include:

- Prioritizing privacy: Designing products and services that respect users' privacy and offer them control over their personal data can help build trust and create a more secure digital environment.
- Ensuring user well-being: Considering the mental and emotional well-being of users when designing

experiences, such as limiting addictive features or creating tools that promote healthy digital habits, can help mitigate the negative impact of technology on mental health.

- Addressing unintended consequences: Being mindful of the potential negative consequences of your designs and working to minimize any harm they may cause, such as reducing the spread of misinformation or mitigating algorithmic biases, can help create a more responsible tech ecosystem.

As you continue your journey as a UX designer, remember that your work has the potential to touch the lives of countless individuals. By embracing the UX designer mindset and focusing on making a positive impact through your designs, you can contribute to a better, more connected, and more empathetic world.

In the end, the journey of lifelong learning and growth as a UX designer is about more than just advancing your own career. It's about using your skills and expertise to create meaningful change in the world around you. Keep pushing yourself to learn, adapt, and innovate, and you'll continue to make an impact through UX design, one user experience at a time.

Milton Keynes UK
Ingram Content Group UK Ltd.
UKHW032156170724
445718UK00004B/31

9 798223 716549